STEP IT UP
KNITS

STEP IT UP KNITS

Take Your Skills to the Next Level
with 25 Quick and Stylish Projects

....

VICKIE HOWELL

photographs by Jody Horton

CHRONICLE BOOKS

SAN FRANCISCO

Library of Congress Cataloging-in-Publication Data

Howell, Vickie.
  Step it up knits : take your skills to the next level with 25 quick and stylish projects /
Vickie Howell. — 1 [edition].
    pages cm
  ISBN 978-1-4521-0663-2 (hardback)
  1. Knitting—Patterns. I. Title.
TT825.H683 2012
746.43'2—dc23
              2012013780

Manufactured in China

Designed by Allison Weiner
Prop styling by Kate LeSueur and Eliza Kelly
Wardrobe styling by Rose Tran

The photographer wishes to thank the entire photo team that worked with him on this
project, especially first assistant Bill Sallans and the farm crew out at Montesino Ranch.

Bernat is a registered trademark of Spinrite Limited Partnership. Berroco Flicker and
Berroco Peruvia are registered trademarks of Berroco, Inc. Blue Sky Alpacas is a regis-
tered trademark of Blue Sky Alpacas, Inc. Boye is a registered trademark of Boye Needle
Co. Madeline-tosh is a registered trademark of Amy Hendrix DBA Madelinetosh Co.

10 9 8 7 6 5 4 3 2 1

Chronicle Books LLC
680 Second Street
San Francisco, California 94107
www.chroniclebooks.com

For my dad, who enabled me to write this book while sitting in a peaceful space with a wilderness view. I hope wherever you are now, you're experiencing "another day in paradise."

CONTENTS ▶ ▶ ▶ ▶ ▶ ▶ ▶ ▶ ▶ ▶ ▶ ▶ ▶ ▶ ▶

▶ ▶ ▶ ▶ ▶ ▶ ▶ ▶ ▶ ▶ ▶ ▶ ▶ ▶ ▶ ▶ ▶

INTRODUCTION ▶ ▶ ▶ ▶ ▶ ▶ ▶ ▶ ▶ ▶ ▶ ▶ ▶

I assume that everyone is as busy as I am—balancing home, parenthood, career, and whenever possible, creative fulfillment. Finding time to be creative can be tough sometimes. In the stolen moments of a busy knitter's life—needles in hand, clicking away in line at the grocery store, on the sidelines of a kid's game, or at the office during lunch break—it's often difficult to fathom finding the time and brain space to make more than a ribbed scarf or a stockinette beanie. The pure commitment needed to knit a complex Fair Isle sweater, a multicabled coat, or an intricate lace shawl can seem so daunting that it's tempting to just never try.

But, my frazzled friends, there's no need to settle. You can brush up on skills, learn new techniques, and up your overall stitching skill ante while making beautiful yet absolutely doable projects in the process. You can have your yarn-y cake and knit it, too! The trick is to make small projects that pack enough punch to challenge you, but not so much that you'll need to lock yourself in a closet just to finish one row. Like with everything else in life, you can find a balance in your knitting so it fits into your own life.

This book features patterns for twenty-five quick-to-knit accessories, especially designed to take beginning knitters to the intermediate level while still being engaging enough for the more advanced knitter. Each pattern will require a few higher level skills to complete, but will be backed up by a comprehensive techniques section at the front of the book to guide you. We'll discover a love of lace, go cuckoo for cables, get into intarsia, step lightly into short rows, fawn over felting, and so much more!

▶ ▶ ▶ ▶　▶ ▶ ▶ ▶ ▶ ▶ ▶ ▶ ▶　▶ ▶ ▶ ▶　▶ ▶ ▶ ▶ ▶

Stepping up your knitting skills doesn't just mean learning new tricks, though. It's also about boosting your confidence so you can figure out what a pattern means and intuitively solve problems on your own. To that end, many patterns within these pages have been written in a less rudimentary style than you might find in a beginner's book. I use lots of abbreviations, give multiple directions at once, leave out some row-by-row stitch counts when they're unnecessary focal points (because sometimes if you're off by a stitch one way or another, it won't really matter), and don't spell out reverse shaping for you. These challenges will be good for you, will help you build your skills, and I promise I'll be gentle. No worries: If you get stuck, the Terms & Abbreviations and the Techniques sections will give you a hand.

It's my hope that each knitted project in this book will teach you something new and offer you a sense of accomplishment. If you pick up a new technique or two and end up with a finished project (or twenty-five), then my job is done. I believe in you. Knit forward, knit on!

Nikie

TERMS & ABBREVIATIONS ▶ ▶ ▶ ▶ ▶ ▶ ▶ ▶

beg begin(s); beginning

bk1 brioche knit stitch
(Knit together the slipped stitch and yarn over.)

BO bind off (cast off)

bp1 brioche purl stitch
(Purl together the slipped stitch and yarn over.)

cb cable back

CC contrasting color

cf cable front

ch chain

circ(s) circular needle(s)

cn cable needle

CO cast on

cont continue, continuing

dec(s) decrease (k2tog is best choice unless noted otherwise), decreasing

dpn(s) double-pointed needle(s)

est established

inc(s) increase (M1 is best choice unless otherwise noted)

join connect for working in the round

k knit

k2tog knit 2 stitches together as one stitch

k2tog-tbl knit 2 stitches together through the back loops

kf&b knit into the front and back loop of same stitch

ktbl knit stitch through the back loop

LC left slanting cable

LPC left cable with purl stitches in between

m marker/stitch marker

M1 make 1 (increase 1) stitch
(Using the RH needle to pick up loop at the base of the next stitch on the LH needle, place loop on LH needle. Treat loop as a new stitch and work normally.)

MB make bobble

MC main color

p purl

p2tog purl 2 stitches together

p2tog-tbl purl 2 stitches together through back loop

p4tog purl 4 stitches together
(With yarn in front, insert right-hand needle into next 4 stitches.)

patt pattern

pm place marker

prep prepare, preparation

psso pass slipped stitch over purlwise (Purl all 4 stitches together. You'll then have a triple decrease.)

RC right slanting cable

rem remaining

rep repeat, repeating

rev reverse, reversing

rev St st reverse stockinette stitch

rib ribbing

rnd(s) round(s)

RPC right cable with purl stitches in between

RS right side

RT right twist

s2kp slip 2 stitches together, knit 1, pass the 2 slipped stitches over

sc single crochet

skp slip 1 knitwise, knit 1, pass the slipped stitch over

sl slip

sl-w-t slip, wrap, turn

ssk slip, slip, knit

ssp slip 2 sts knitwise, one at a time, to RH needle (Slip them both purlwise back to LH needle. Purl them together through their back loops.)

st(s) stitch(es)

St st stockinette stitch

tbl through the back loop

waste yarn scrap yarn

work even work in pattern without increasing or decreasing any stitches

WS wrong side

wyib with yarn in back

wyif with yarn in front

yb yarn back

yf yarn forward

yo yarn over

* starting (or ending) point to repeat instructions

rep from * repeat all the instructions following the asterisk

rep ** repeat the instructions between the asterisks

TECHNIQUES
MOVING ON UP

·······················

All techniques used in the projects in this book are illustrated here with step-by-step instructions and photography. Turn to this section as often as you need to, and you'll be an accomplished knitter in no time!

BASIC CABLE LEFT ▶ ▶ ▶ ▶ ▶ ▶ ▶ ▶ ▶ ▶
(A.K.A. CABLE FRONT/CF)

a   b   c

note: Patterns will call for varying widths of cables, but the technique for knitting them is basically the same. Just keep in mind that the number given for the cable (for example, CF6 or 6-st CF) is the total number of stitches for the cable.

On a right-side row, slip the number of cable stitches designated in the pattern onto a cable needle, letting that needle fall in front of the work (a).

Knit the designated number of stitches not on the cable needle (b).

Knit the stitches off the cable needle (you'll probably need to let the left-hand needle drop so that you can work with the cable needle for these stitches) (c).

BASIC CABLE RIGHT ▶ ▶ ▶ ▶ ▶ ▶ ▶ ▶ ▶ ▶ ▶
(A.K.A. CABLE BACK/CB)

a   b   c

On a right-side row, slip the number of cable stitches designated in the pattern onto a cable needle, letting that needle fall to the back of the work (a).

Knit the designated number of stitches not on the cable needle (b).

Knit the stitches off of the cable needle (you'll probably need to let the left-hand needle drop so that you can work with the cable needle for these stitches) (c).

BLOCKING ▶ ▶ ▶ ▶ ▶ ▶ ▶ ▶ ▶ ▶ ▶

To block your knitted piece, lay it out on an ironing board, carpeted floor, or even a table with several layers of towels taped to it. (Basically, you just need a flat surface that can handle a little moisture and some sewing pins.) Arrange the piece smoothly in the size and shape called for in the pattern's schematic. Carefully pin the pieces into place.

Using Mist:
Using a spray bottle on the "mist" setting, dampen the piece(s).

Using Steam:
Move an iron slowly over your project about 4 to 6 in/10 to 15 cm above the piece, using the steam setting to dampen it. Do not place the iron directly on the knitted fabric. Let dry overnight.

BOBBLE STITCH ▶ ▶ ▶ ▶ ▶ ▶ ▶ ▶ ▶ ▶ ▶ ▶

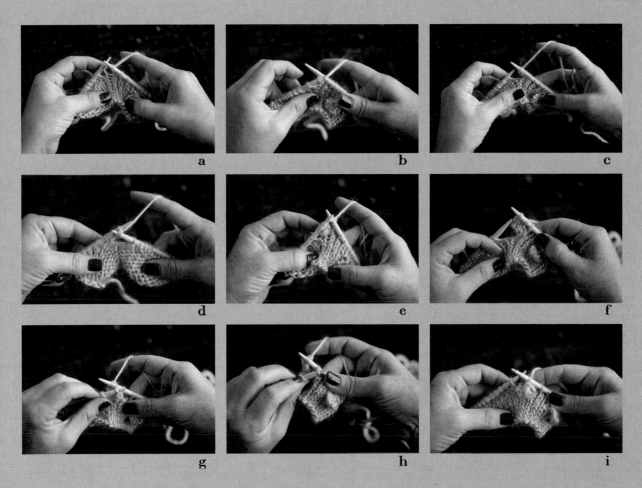

Knit in the front (a) and back (b) of one stitch, three times, so you have 6 stitches on the RH needle (c).

Turn your work, and purl those 6 stitches (d).

Turn your work again; k2tog three times (e) so you have bobble stitches on the RH needle (f).

Pass the second (g) and third stitches (h), one by one, over the first stitch, letting them drop off the needle (i).

BRIOCHE STITCH ▶▶▶▶▶▶▶▶▶▶▶▶
(TWO COLORS)

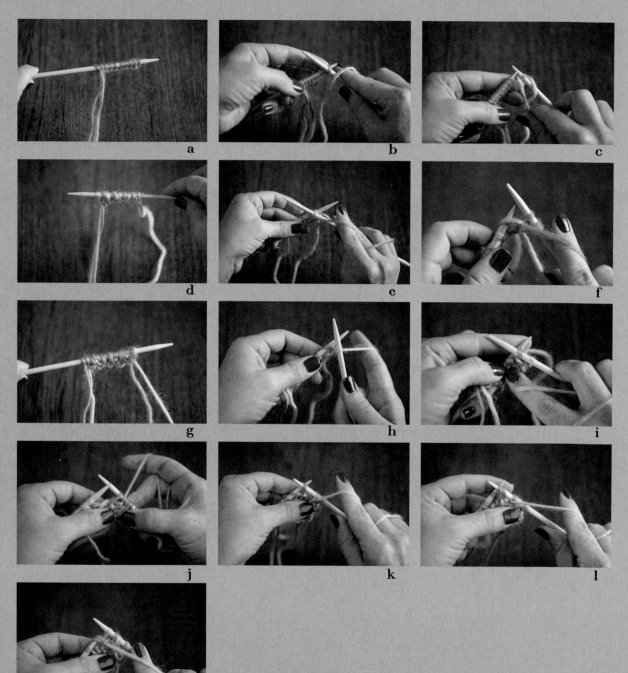

a

b

c

d

e

f

g

h

i

j

k

l

m

Prep Row: (RS CC, forms purl columns in CC on RS) (a).

Slide work to the other tip of the needle and attach CC, wyif (b), *sl 1 (c), yo, p1; rep from *.

Turn work (d).

Row 1: (WS MC, forms purl columns in MC) Wyif, *sl 1 (e), yo, bp1 (f) (brioche purl—purl together the slipped stitch and yo from row before); rep from * (g). Do not turn work.

Row 1: (WS CC, forms knit columns in CC) Slide work to other tip of needle where CC is hanging. With CC, *bk1 (brioche knit—knit together the slipped stitch and yo from row before) (h), yf s sl 1, yo (i); rep from *. Turn work.

Row 2: (RS MC, forms knit columns in MC) Maintain the CC yo of last worked st by holding it under left needle to the back, with MC, *bk1, yf (j), sl 1, yo; rep from *. Do not turn work.

Row 2: (RS CC, forms purl columns in CC) Slide work to other tip of needle where CC is hanging. With CC, wyif, *sl 1, yo (k), bp1 (l, m); rep from *. Turn work.

CIRCULAR 3-NEEDLE BIND-OFF ▶ ▶ ▶ ▶

Hold circ ends parallel so half of the sts are on one side of the needle and half on the other side. Using an additional needle, bind off 2 sts (1 on front needle, 1 on back) at a time by knitting them together; repeat. There will now be 2 sts on the additional needle; bring the second st over the first to drop off the needle. Repeat to end.

CROCHET CHAIN ▶ ▶ ▶ ▶ ▶ ▶ ▶ ▶ ▶ ▶ ▶ ▶

a

b

c

d

Tie a slipknot onto a crochet hook (a).

Wrap the yarn counterclockwise around the hook (b) and pull through the loop on the hook (c).

Continue in this manner (d) until your chain is the desired length.

tip: It helps to hold the tail of the yarn securely between your thumb and middle finger while you're working!

DROPPING STITCHES ▶▶▶▶▶▶▶▶▶▶

a   b

Once you get to the place in your project where you'd like the dropped stitch to start from, let the intended stitch fall off of your needle (a) and gently tug on the knitted fabric (b) until that stitch unravels in a ladder effect and reaches the bottom edge.

EYELET STITCH ▶▶▶▶▶▶▶▶▶▶▶▶

Eyelets are created by working a series of yos and k2togs.

To yo, bring working yarn to the front and knit stitch normally. This will wrap the yarn around the needle, creating a yarn over.

To k2tog, insert RH needle up through 2 stitches on the LH needle and knit them together.

I-CORD ▷ ▷ ▷ ▷ ▷ ▷ ▷ ▷ ▷ ▷ ▷ ▷ ▷

a   b   c

With dpns or circ, cast on stitches. Knit across row. Once that row is complete (a), slide the stitches to the opposite end of the needle, and switch hands so that the needle (or end, if you are working on a circ) with the knit row is in your left hand.

The working yarn will appear to be at the wrong end of the row, but just bring it behind the stitches and begin knitting again (b).

The strand of yarn stretched across the back will create a cording effect. Continue in this manner (c) until you achieve an I-cord of the desired length.

INTARSIA ▷ ▷ ▷ ▷ ▷ ▷ ▷ ▷ ▷ ▷ ▷ ▷ ▷

Work in main color, switching to pattern color(s) as called for by chart. When changing from one ball of yarn to another, make sure to wrap the yarn you are currently using around the next yarn you are going to use to avoid holes in the fabric. Don't worry if while you're knitting your garment doesn't seem to be lying perfectly flat. With intarsia projects, blocking usually fixes any misshaping that occurs.

KITCHENER STITCH ▶▶▶▶▶▶▶▶▶▶

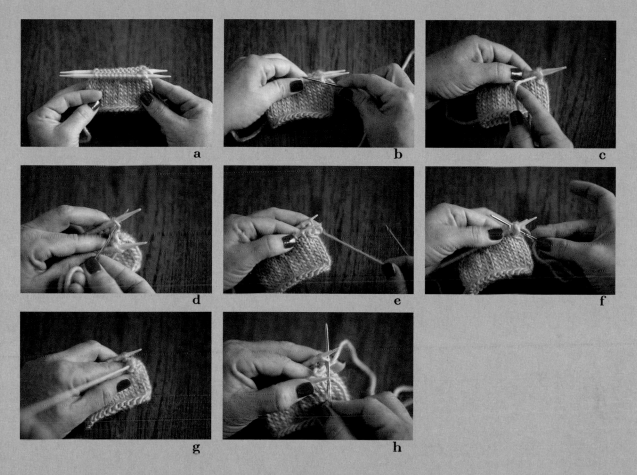

Place an even amount of front piece stitches on one needle and back piece stitches on another (a). Hold the needles in one hand, parallel to each other with wrong sides facing.

Using your other hand and a yarn needle threaded with the tail of the working yarn cut after the knitting portion was finished, come through the first stitch on the front needle purlwise (b), leaving it on the needle (c).

Then, come through the first stitch on the back needle knitwise (d), also leaving it on the needle. These two steps have created a stable start.

*Come through the first stitch on the *front* needle knitwise, letting it drop off the needle (e); come through the next stitch on the *front* needle purlwise (f), leaving it on the needle.

Come through the first stitch on the *back* needle purlwise, letting it fall off the needle (g).

Come through the next stitch on the *back* needle knitwise (h), leaving it on the needle; repeat from * until finished.

KNITTING IN THE ROUND ▶ ▶ ▶ ▶ ▶ ▶
WITH A CIRCULAR NEEDLE

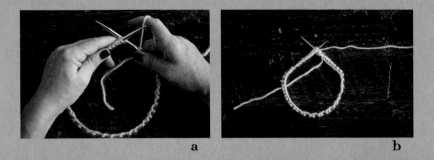

a   b

Once you've cast on the appropriate number of stitches on a circ, join the round by holding the needle end with the working yarn in your right hand and the other end in your left (a).

Knit 1 stitch. Once you've done that, lay your circ down on a flat surface and make sure that the stitches aren't twisted (b). If you can run your finger all the way around the inner part of the circle only touching the bottom part of the stitches (not the loop part), then you're good to go. Continue knitting the round. If you find the stitches are in fact twisted, undo the stitch you've just knit, straighten out the stitches with your fingers, and try again. The tail will signify the beginning of the round, but you may also want to pm there as a reminder.

KNITTING IN THE ROUND ▶ ▶ ▶ ▶ ▶ ▶ ▶
WITH DOUBLE-POINTED NEEDLES

a

b

c

d

Once you've cast on the required number of stitches on dpns and evenly dispersed them over 3 needles (a), lay the needles down on a flat surface, forming a triangle.

The needles can now be numbered 1, 2, and 3, starting with the one *farthest* away from the working yarn. As with knitting in the round on a circ, the most important thing about joining the round is making sure that the stitches aren't twisted; all of the loops should be on the inner edge of your triangle. Once you've checked on them, you're ready to join the round by introducing your fourth needle (b).

To do this, hold your triangle in your left hand with needle 3 on the right side. Insert needle 4 into the first stitch on needle 1 and knit it, using the working yarn from 3 (c). The first stitch is always the trickiest to accomplish, so don't worry if you don't get it on the first try!

Once you've knit that first stitch, your round is joined. Next, pm and knit (or work whatever stitch called for in the pattern) all the way across the first needle. The needle in your left hand will now be empty. Switch the empty needle to your right hand and begin working the stitches on the second needle (d). Continue in this manner until you've worked the stitches off all the needles.

MACHINE FELTING ▶▶ ▶ ▶ ▶ ▶ ▶ ▶ ▶

Place the knitted project in a zippered pillowcase or finely meshed bag. Put the bag into the washing machine along with an old pair of jeans or a towel, to contribute to the agitation, and wash the item on hot, excluding the spin portion of the washing cycle. Repeat as many times as necessary to achieve the desired felting result. Take care to check on your project every 5 minutes or so. When finished, squeeze excess water out of project, shape with your hands per pattern instructions, and let dry on a towel. Keep in mind that felting will only work with natural, animal fibers that *have not* been "superwash" treated. Oh, and front-loading washers will not felt garments, because they don't agitate.

MATTRESS STITCH ▶▶ ▶ ▶ ▶ ▶ ▶ ▶ ▶

a   b   c

With the RS facing you on a table, lay the two knitted pieces that you want to seam together side by side. If you pull slightly on the edge of one of your pieces, you'll notice a row of bars between the stitches.

Thread a yarn needle with yarn, and come up through the back edge of one of your pieces (a).

Then go under one of the bars and pull the yarn through. Repeat the last step on your second piece (b).

You'll notice your edges slowly beginning to fold inward, creating an almost invisible seam. Continue in this manner (c) until finished. Securely weave in ends.

MITERED SQUARES ▶▶▶▶▶▶▶▶▶
(SHAPING)

Mitering is a simple method of creating a right angle in knitting. It can be used to shape things like necklines and borders or, like in Squared Up (page 87), to turn a straight line into a square. Here's how:

Pm at the center point of the sts on your needle.

Row 1: (RS) Knit to 2 sts before marker, k2tog-tbl, sl marker, k2tog, k to end.

Row 2: Knit.

Join MC.

Repeat Rows 1 and 2.

Continue as est, repeating 2 row stripes, until 2 sts remain.

BO last 2 sts on WS row.

MOSAIC KNITTING ▶▶▶▶▶▶▶▶▶

Mosiac knitting involves two different colors of yarn, only one of which is actually used to knit with per row. The only time you change yarns is at the beginning of every other row, like you would if you were knitting two row stripes. Following written directions and starting on the right side of your project, knit with the designated color while slipping the secondary colored stitches purlwise. Repeat this process on the wrong side. Reverse the process for the next two rows. Continue as est, following written instructions and switching working yarn every other row until pattern is finished.

NEEDLE FELTING ▶ ▶ ▶ ▶ ▶ ▶ ▶ ▶ ▶ ▶ ▶

a

Place foam under felt piece, directly under where you want to add your felted stencil design.

Lay out your stencil; once you're satisfied with its placement, use a felting needle to lightly stab a small amount of roving into place (a). Take care to hold stencil in place with one hand while you're needle felting with the other.

Slowly begin adding more roving, making sure the fiber is situated exactly where you'd like it.

Finally, stab the roving repeatedly, permanently attaching it to the project. Repeat this process until the design is complete.

PICOT BIND-OFF ▶ ▶ ▶ ▶ ▶ ▶ ▶ ▶ ▶ ▶ ▶

a   **b**   **c**

K1, place stitch back on left-hand needle (a), CO 2 stitches (b), BO 4 stitches.

*Slip stitch on right-hand needle back onto left-hand needle, CO 2 stitches, BO 4 (c).
Repeat from * to end.

READING A CHART ▶▶▶▶▶▶▶▶▶

A chart is provided in the pattern any time there's a motif to be knitted into your piece, whether it's a stitch design or a color work design. To read a chart for projects worked on straight needles, simply start at the bottom and follow along from right to left for RS rows and from left to right for WS rows. If you're working in the round, you'll read every round from right to left. That's all there is to it!

SINGLE-CROCHET EDGING ▶▶▶▶▶▶▶

a

b

c

d

Tie a slipknot onto the crochet hook. Insert the hook into the front loop of the knitted edge stitch that you'd like to embellish. You'll now have two loops (stitches) on your hook. Wrap yarn counterclockwise around hook and draw it through the first loop (a). Wrap yarn counterclockwise once more, and draw through both loops.

Insert the hook into the next knit stitch. Wrap the yarn and draw it through first loop (b) and then wrap the yarn again and draw it through both loops (c).

Continue in this manner (d) until edging is complete.

SHORT-ROW HEEL TURN ▶ ▶ ▶ ▶ ▶ ▶ ▶ ▶ ▶

a

b

c

d

e

f

g

h

i

j

The heel of a sock is worked on 50 percent of the sock's overall stitches. It's time to turn the heel so that the foot portion can point at a 90-degree angle from the back of the heel, once your heel flap has been worked to form a square. To do that, you employ what's called a short row, which means to work partial rows at different intervals to create depth or shape to a flat knitted piece.

Using the stitch count (28) from the Sock It to Me socks (page 63), here are the steps of turning a heel with the short-row method I use:

Row 1: (RS) Sl 1 (a), k15 (b), ssk (c), k1, turn (d).

Row 2: Sl 1, p6 (e), p2tog, p1, turn.

Row 3: Sl 1 (f), k7 (g), ssk, k1, turn.

Row 4: Sl 1, p8 (h), p2tog (i), p1, turn.

Continue in this manner, slipping the first st, working to the 1 st before gap, and working sts before and after the gap tog, until all heel sts are worked (j)—18 sts rem.

PROJECTS

LEARN IT, MAKE IT

HAND OVER TWIST

CABLED HAND WARMERS

....

Anyone who uses their hands a lot can surely use a pair of Cabled Hand Warmers while working during the chilly months. And frankly, hand warmers just look cool with a winter outfit. One of the easiest ways to create a place for your thumb when making hand or wrist warmers is to simply go from working the piece in the round to back and forth for a couple of inches. In this project, you'll also add a cable and practice following a chart while switching from rounds to rows. Consider your skills stepped up!

Instructions

right hand warmer

cuff

With dpns, CO 36(40) sts. Distribute evenly over dpns as follows:
needle 1, 8(10) sts; needle 2, 20(20) sts; needle 3, 8(10) sts. Join,
taking care not to twist.

Work in k2, p2 rib for 2(2½) in/5(6) cm.

body

Begin cable chart over 20 sts on needle 2, while working sts on
needles 1 and 3 in rev St st.

Work 12 rnds of chart in this manner.

Cont as est, working Rnds 1–10 of chart.

From here, you'll stop working in the rnd and will work in rows to
create the thumbhole.

thumbhole (between needles 2 and 3):

Next row (Row 11 of chart): Work stitches on needles 1 and 2 as est.
Turn piece, with WS facing. Work Row 12 of chart on needle 2, then
cont to end in rev St st on needles 1 and 3. Turn.

Cont in rows, work Rows 1–12 of chart once on needle 2, maintaining
rev St st background on rem needles. Switch back to working in the rnd.

Next row (begins on needle 3): Purl sts on needle 3 to get you back to
beg of rnd.

Next rnd: Rejoin round; work in k2, p2 rib for 1 in/2.5 cm more.

BO in rib patt.

left hand warmer

Work as for right hand warmer, rev thumbhole opening when working
back and forth.

finishing

Using yarn needle, weave in ends.

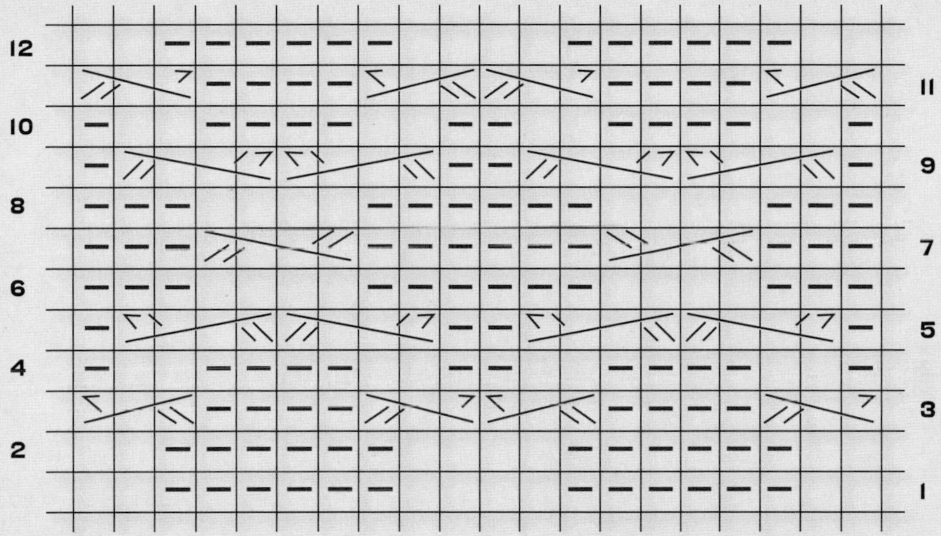

STITCH KEY

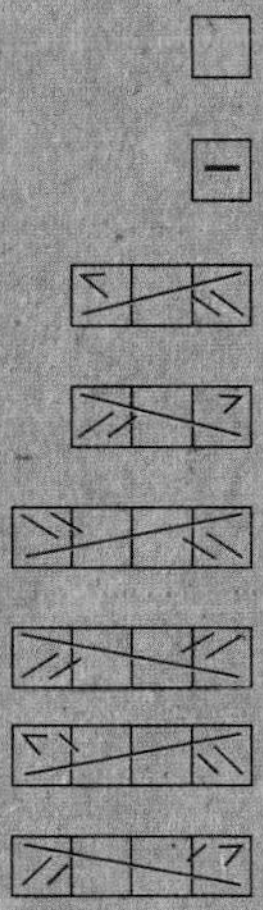

☐ k on RS, p on WS

— p on RS, k on WS

3-st RPC

3-st LPC

4-st RC

4-st LC

4-st RPC

4-st LPC

BOB(BLE) AND WEAVE

BOBBLE STITCH MITTENS

·····················

Mittens make great gifts, and are also perfect little canvases for trying out different stitches because they are small and easy. With Bob(ble) and Weave, you'll practice reading a basic chart while stitching decorative bobbles. I knitted these mittens up in a chartreuse wool-blend yarn that makes a stylish statement while keeping your fingers toasty.

Instructions

right mitten

cuff

With smaller dpns, CO 36(40) sts. Distribute stitches over 3 dpns as
follows: Needle 1, 9(11) sts; needle 2, 18(18) sts; needle 3: 9(11) sts.
Join, taking care not to twist.
Work in k2, p2 rib for 3(3½) in/7.5(9) cm.
Switch to larger dpns.

body

Knit 1 rnd.
Setup Rnd: Needle 1: K9(11); needle 2: work Row 1 of chart (see
pages 40–41) over 18 sts; needle 3: k9(11).
Cont in this manner, work 2 rnds even, working sts on needles 1 and
3 in St st, and Rows 2 and 3 of chart on needle 2.

thumb gore

Cont 12-row chart patt on needle 2, shape thumb gore on needle 3 (for
right mitten) or needle 1 (for left mitten) as follows:
Rnd 4: K1 (this will now be considered the first thumb st), pm, M1,
M1, pm, k1 (last thumb st), work to end of needle 3 (right mitten) or
needle 1 (left mitten).
Work 2 rnds even, working Rnds 5 and 6 of chart on needle 2.
Cont in patt, rep last 3 rounds (increasing 2 sts between markers)
4(5) times total—12(14) thumb sts.
Slip thumb sts onto waste yarn to place on hold.
Resume working in the round on rem 34(38) body sts. Cont with chart,
as est, until piece measures 8(8½) in/20(21.5) cm from edge of cuff.

top shaping

Next rnd: Discontinue chart; work all sts in St st.
Rnd 1: (dec rnd) *K2tog, k3; rep from * around.
Rnds 2, 4, and 6: Knit.
Rnd 3: (dec rnd) *K2tog, k2; rep from * around.
Rnd 5: (dec rnd) *K2tog; rep from * around—10 sts rem.
Break yarn, leaving a 6 in/15 cm tail.
Weave yarn through live 10 sts and draw closed.

thumb

Slip 12(14) sts from waste yarn onto dpns. Using needle 3, pick up 3 sts
    at thumb gap; pm. Divide stitches evenly among needles—15(17) sts.
Knit rounds until thumb measures 2(2½) in/5(6) cm from pick-up rnd.

thumb shaping

Rnd 1: (dec rnd) *K1, k2tog; rep from * around—10(12) sts rem.
Rnds 2 and 4: Knit.
Rnd 3: (dec rnd) *K2tog; rep from * around—5(7) sts rem.
Finish as for mitten top.

left mitten

Work as for right mitten, using Left Mitten chart and reversing thumb
    placement.

tip: Be sure to check your stitches to make sure they're snug,
especially after the bobble stitch and for the thumb. A hole-y mitten
makes for a chilly hand!

finishing

Using yarn needle, weave in ends. Block if necessary.

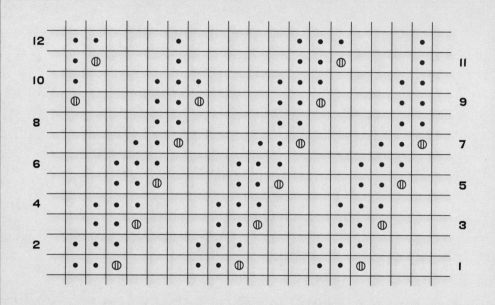

LEFT MITTEN

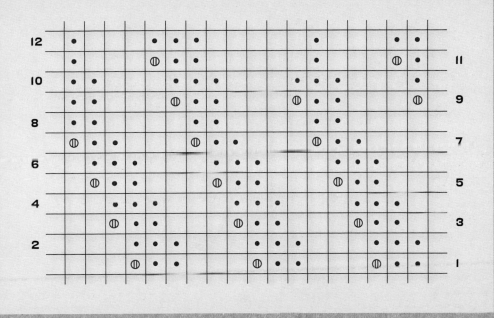

RIGHT MITTEN

STITCH KEY

☐ Knit

• Purl

Ⓜ Bobble

Earth's land surface. An exact figure is tricky because of numerous offshore islands and disputes over exactly where Europe ends and Asia begins. Both Russia and Turkey, for instance, have one foot in the dock and one foot in the boat, so to speak. But the Europe... states—including less familiar little places like Monaco, Andorra, San Marino, and Vatican City—hold more than 25 percent of the world's population.

An exact count of Europe's separate states has been made some... what tricky in the past year or two. And it's gotten difficult to tel... the players and the breakup of the Soviet Union, there are now at least many and forty separate states in Europe, depending on what you call state... and what you call Europe—and they're not done making new coun... tries yet!

Even as Europe is moving toward a unified system of currencies, an end to protective tariffs, and the opening of borders—making national passports obsolete within the continent... the entire conti... nent has been gripped by new waves of ferv... nationalism. Initially, that nationalism wa... a minimum of bloodshed as the astonish... ope and later the Soviet Union were pla... in several ethnic, religious, and t... ries-old years of authoritarian Co... shed to Europe since... to Europe up int... aks Europe as once a...

urope: A... and

Spain
Finland
Though, not actually, one of the Scandinavian countries, Fin... land is culturally and politically considered to be a part of this group.

Low Countries
Belgium
Luxembourg
The Netherlands
In 1958, these three countries made an economic union, called Benelux, a convenient reminder of their names.

The Iberian Peninsula
Portugal
Spain

Alpine States
Austria
France
Italy
Liechtenstein
Switzerland

...ence of the post-Soviet era, Yugoslavia has... ween rival ethnic groups. To date... st of the ashes of World War I has been... er republics. The new Yugoslavia, much... ics of the former regions of Serbia and Mon... s of the old Yugoslavia have been recognized as... lics. They are Slovenia, Croatia, Bosnia and Her... acedonia.

131

MO' WARMERS

MOSAIC WRIST WARMERS

....

Colorful wrist warmers are a terrific way to add a pop to an otherwise drab winter outfit. And in my humble opinion, mosaic knitting is one of the most user-friendly color work options. You don't need to carry multiple yarns across your rows or worry about creating holes by changing yarns between color blocks. Basically, the technique garners big results with minimal effort. These Mo' Warmers are cozy-cute and will show the world you have mo' knitting skills for sure!

SKILLS
Mosaic Knitting (page 25)
Thumb Gore
Knitting in the Round with
Double-Pointed Needles
(page 23)

SIZE
Women's M

**FINISHED
MEASUREMENTS**
Circumference: 8 in/20.5 cm
Length: 10 in/25.5 cm

YARN
Vickie Howell Sheep(ish)
for Bernat (70% acrylic/
30% wool; 167 yd/153 m):
Turquoise(ish) (MC), White(ish)
(CC), 1 ball each
or substitute any worsted-
weight (#4) wool blend

NEEDLES
1 set US 7/4.5 mm
double-pointed needles (or
size needed to obtain gauge)
1 set US 8/5 mm
double-pointed needles (or size
larger than the smaller needles)

NOTIONS
Markers
Waste yarn
Yarn needle

GAUGE
18 stitches and 22 rows per
4 in/10 cm in St st on
smaller needles

Instructions (make 2)

cuff

With smaller dpns and MC, CO 36 sts. Join round, taking care not
to twist.
Work in k2, p2 rib for 1 in/2.5 cm.
Switch to larger needles for working the next round.

body

Rnd 1: With MC, Knit.
Rnd 2: Purl.
Rnds 3–4: With CC, k1, *sl 1, k2; rep from * around.
Rnds 5–6: With MC, rep Rnds 1 and 2.
Rnds 7–8: With CC, *k3, sl 1; rep from * around.
Rep Rnds 1–8 until piece measures 6 in/15 cm from CO edge.

mosaic
note: Always CO with the color of yarn opposite of what you're going
to knit for your first row of stitches.

thumb gore
note: All sts between markers will be worked in 2-round stripe
pattern to correspond with color being worked in mosaic pattern
stitch for body.

Work 18 sts in est patt, pm, M1, k1, M1, pm, work in est patt around.
Next rnd: Continue in est pattern to marker, sl marker, k to next marker,
sl marker, work in est patt around.
Next rnd: Work as est to marker, sl marker, M1, k to next marker, M1,
sl marker, work as est around.
Next rnd: Continue in est pattern to marker, sl marker, k to next marker,
sl marker, work in est pattern around.
Repeat last 2 rounds, until there are 11 sts between markers—47 sts.
Next rnd: Work in est pattern to thumb, remove markers and place
11 thumb sts on waste yarn, work as est around.
Work 7 more rnds even in est st patt.

Cut CC.
With MC and smaller needles, work in k2, p2 rib for 1 in/2.5 cm.
BO in rib.

thumb shaping
With MC, place 11 thumb sts on 3 of the smaller sized dpns. Pick up
   1 st over gap and join—12 sts.
Next 2 rnds: Knit.
Work in k2, p2 rib for 3 rnds.
BO in rib.

finishing

Using a yarn needle, weave in ends.

URBAN KICKS

BABY BOOTIES

These baby booties are made for walkin'! With their ribbed cuff and faux-suede sole, your baby will be warm and stylin' through the winter months. In this project, you'll work with fabric form soles; master a simple, ribbed cuff; and step up your skills with an I-cord bind-off. There's nothing cuter than a kiddo in cute kicks!

Instructions (make 2)

cuff

CO 16.
Rows 1–3: Knit.
Row 4: Purl.
Repeat rows 1–4 until piece measures 5½ in/14 cm from CO edge.
Knit 2 more rows.

I-cord button-loop BO

BO 4, *K1 (2 sts on RH needle), leave the rest of the sts hanging (on
hold) on LH needle. Hold needle with 2 sts in left hand, and pick up
spare needle with right hand. Work 2-st I-cord for 1½ in/4 cm (or until
long enough to fit around chosen button). BO I-cord, leaving tail for
sewing. Let hang. BO next 3 sts; rep from * twice more.

note: Last I-cord will be worked on last 2 sts.

edging

Pick up 28 sts evenly along one side of cuff piece.
Work in k1, p1 rib for 6 rows. BO in rib.

finishing

Using yarn needle and tails, sew button loops in place.
Following bootie manufacturer's instructions, hand-sew long
(nonribbed) side of cuff to inside of bootie.
Sew on buttons to correspond with button loops.

BOOT LEGGED

SEED RIB BOOT SOCKS

....

I love how a good, tall sock adds a little peek of knitted color (while keeping your foot comfy) under this season's favorite boot. This project pairs self-striping yarn with a seed-stitch rib that will give a little texture, while hugging the foot. Boot Legged will have your feet feeling fancy, and your sock skill ante officially stepped-up!

SKILLS
Knitting in the Round with
Double-Pointed Needles
(page 23)
Short-Row Heel Turn
(pages 28–29)
Kitchener Stitch (page 21)

SIZE
Woman's M

FINISHED
MEASUREMENTS
Foot Circumference: 8 in/20 cm
Cuff length: 10 in/25 cm

YARN
Noro Taiyo Scott (50% cotton,
17% wool, 17% nylon, 16% silk;
462 yd/425 m per 100 g):
01 multi, 1 ball

NEEDLES
1 set US 2/2.75 mm double-
pointed needles (or size
needed to obtain gauge)

NOTIONS
Yarn needle
Stitch holder

GAUGE
28 stitches and 40 rows per
4 in/10 cm in stockinette
stitch

Instructions (make 2)

Beginning at upper edge, CO 54 sts. Divide sts evenly over 3 dpns. Join, taking care not to twist. Begin Seed Rib:

Round 1: *K3, p1, k2; repeat from * around.

Round 2: *P1, k5; repeat from * around.

Repeat Rounds 1 and 2 until leg measures 10 in/25 cm from CO edge.

turn heel

Place 27 sts on 1 needle for heel. Place remaining 27 instep sts on holder, making a note of last round of Seed Rib worked, and continue as follows, working back and forth in rows on heel stitches only:

Row 1 (RS): Sl st, k1; repeat from * across.

Row 2: Sl st 1, purl to end.

Repeat these 2 rows 15 times, or until heel flap is square.

heel

Row 1 (RS): Sl 1, k15, ssk, k1, turn.

Row 2: Sl 1, p6, p2tog, p1, turn.

Row 3: Sl 1, k7, ssk, k1, turn.

Row 4: Sl 1, p8, p2tog, p1, turn.

Continue in this manner, slipping first st, working to 1 st before gap, then working sts before and after gap together, until all heel sts are worked. 17 sts remain.

gusset

set up round

Needle 1: Knit heel sts, then pick up and knit 13 sts along side of heel. 30 stitches on needle 1.

Needle 2: Working across 27 instep sts, keeping first and last 3 sts in St st, k3, work next round of Seed Rib across to last 3 sts, end k3.

Needle 3: Pick up and knit 13 sts along side of heel, knit first 9 sts of heel. Pm for beginning of round (rounds beg and end at this point). 22 stitches on needle 3, 21 stitches on needle 1.

round 1
Needle 1: Knit to last 3 sts of needle, k2tog, k1.
Needle 2: Work in Seed Rib pattern across instep sts, keeping first and last
   3 stitches in St st.
Needle 3: K1, ssk, knit to end.

round 2
Work even in pattern est (Seed Rib across instep stitches, St st on remain-
   ing sts).
Repeat Rounds 1 and 2 until 54 sts remain.

foot

Work even in pattern until foot measures 8 in/20 cm.

toe

round 1
Needle 1: Knit to last 3 sts, k2tog, k1.
Needle 2: K1, ssk, knit to last 3 sts, k2tog, k1.
Needle 3: K1, ssk, knit to end of needle.

round 2
Knit.
Repeat Rounds 1 and 2 until 14 sts remain.

finishing

Graft toe using Kitchener Stitch.

LEG BONE

HERRINGBONE RIB LEG WARMERS

....

You can take a project from beginner to intermediate just by altering the stitch pattern a bit. In this project, you'll use a chart while working in the round. At first glance, these leg warmers look like they were knit in basic rib. But when you look closer, you'll see that the ribbing points outward in a pretty herringbone design. It's all in the details!

Instructions

body

CO 48(58) sts on 3 dpns. Distribute stitches evenly over the needles.
   Join, taking care not to twist.
Work in k2, p2 rib for 2 in/5 cm.
Next rnd: [K2, p2] 2(3) times, pm, [k2, p2] 9 times, pm, [k2, p2]
   to end.
Next rnd: [K2, p2] to first marker, work herringbone rib stitch chart to
   second marker, [k2, p2] to end.
Continue in this manner, working the design panel in the chart
   with a ribbed background, until the piece measures 15 in/38 cm
   from CO edge.
Work in K2, p2 rib for 2 in/5 cm.
BO in rib.

finishing

With yarn needle, weave in ends.

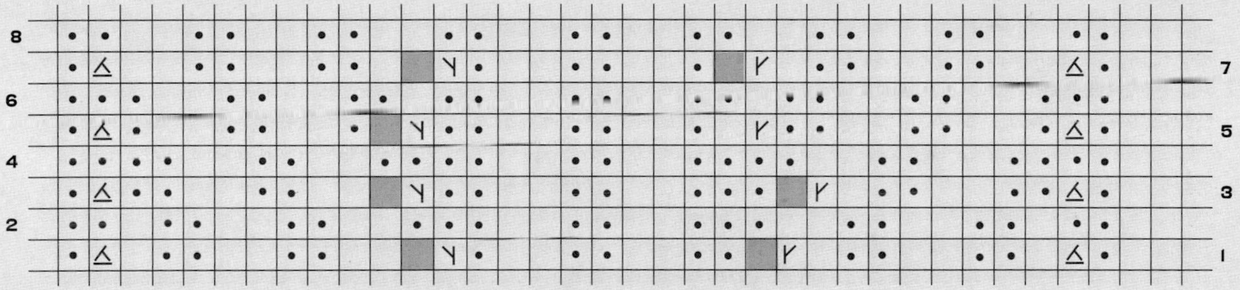

Row numbers left side: 8, 6, 4, 2
Row numbers right side: 7, 5, 3, 1

STITCH KEY

☐	Knit
•	Purl
△	P2tog
Y	Knit in front & back of stitch
⅄	Purl in front & back of stitch
▨	No stitch

FANCY PANTS

LACE CUFF BABY LEGGINGS

....

There's nothing cuter than a newborn baby wearing teeny, tiny pants. Make them in silk and cashmere with lace detailing and your baby will not only be comfortable but also stylish. In this project, you'll practice going from knitting in the round to knitting straight, and adding a simple lace cuff.

SKILLS
Adding Lace Panels
Knitting in the Round with a
Circular Needle (page 22)
Crochet Chain (page 18)
Making a Simple Garment

SIZE
Newborn

FINISHED
MEASUREMENTS
Hips: 13½ in/34 cm
Length: 10 in/25.5 cm

YARN
Sublime Baby Cashmere
Merino Silk DK (75% extra fine
merino/20% silk/
5% cashmere; 127 yd/116 m):
Pansy #0162, 2 balls
or substitute any DK-weight
(#3) silk/wool blend

NEEDLES
US 7/4.5 mm circular needle,
12 in/30.5 cm length (or size
needed to obtain gauge)

NOTIONS
Crochet hook (desired size)
Stitch holder or waste yarn
Yarn needle

GAUGE
20 stitches and 24 rows per
4 in/10 cm in stockinette stitch

Instructions

body

Starting at the top of the leggings and using the circular needle,
CO 68 sts. Join, taking care not to twist.
Rnds 1–3: Knit.
Rnd 4: (picot edging rnd) *Yo, k2tog; rep from * around.
Rnds 5–8: Knit.
Rnd 9: (eyelet rnd) Rep rnd 4.
Continue, working even in St st until piece measures 6 in/15 cm from
eyelet round.

note: From here you'll be working straight (in rows), not in rounds.

right leg
Dividing row: K34, place next 34 sts on stitch holder or waste yarn, turn.
(WS): BO 1, purl to end—33 sts.
(RS): BO 2, k to end—31 sts.
Work even in St st for 2½ in/6 cm more.
Work 10-row lace panel as follows:
Row 1 (RS): *K1, yo, k1, ssk, p1, k2tog, k1, yo, p1, ssk, p1, k2tog, yo,
k1, yo; rep from *, ending with K1.
Row 2: P1, *p4, k1, p1, k1, p3, k1, p4; rep from * to end.
Row 3: *K1, yo, k1, ssk, p1, k2tog, k1, p1, sl 1, k2tog, psso, yo, k3, yo;
rep from *, ending with k1.
Row 4: P1, *p6, k1, p2, k1, p4; rep from * to end.
Row 5: *[K1, yo] twice, ssk, p1, [k2tog] twice, yo, k5, yo; rep from *,
ending with k1.
Row 6: P1, *p7, k1, p1, k1, p5; rep from * to end.
Row 7: *K1, yo, k3, yo, sl 1, k2tog, psso, p1, yo, k1, ssk, p1, k2tog, k1,
yo; rep from *, ending with k1.
Row 8: P1, *[p3, k1] twice, p7; rep from * to end.
Row 9: *K1, yo, k5, yo, ssk, k1, ssk, p1, k2tog, k1, yo; rep from *,
ending with k1.
Row 10: P1, *p3, k1, p2, k1, p8; rep from * to end.
Knit 4 rows.
BO.

left leg

Place 34 held sts on needle, join yarn on WS.

Next Row (WS): BO 2, p to end—32 sts.

Next Row: BO 1, k to end—31 sts rem.

Work as for Right Leg.

> **tip:** For a masculine pant, skip the lace panel and work legs in garter stitch for 5 in/12.5 cm after dividing row.

finishing

Using a yarn needle and yarn, seam together inseam of leggings.

Fold over top edge of leggings at picot rnd to create edging. Use yarn and yarn needle to sew hem down.

Weave in ends.

Create tie by crocheting a 33-in/84-cm (or desired length) chain. Weave tie through eyelet rnd.

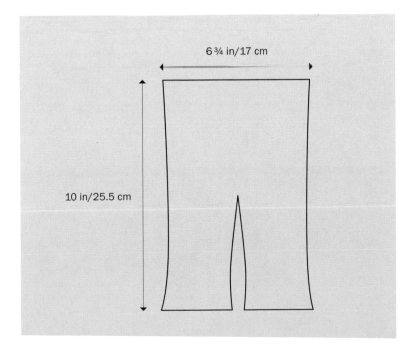

SOCK IT TO ME

LACE CUFF ANKLE SOCKS

....

Sometimes it's the little things that make a project stand out. Here, a sweet, 7-round lace cuff turns an otherwise plain sock into something special. Pair these with some funky platforms or vintage heels and you'll be too cute, to boot!

SKILLS
Knitting in the Round with Double-Pointed Needles (page 23)

Short-Row Heel Turn (pages 28–29)

Kitchener Stitch (page 21)

SIZE
Women's M

FINISHED MEASUREMENTS
Foot circumference: 8 in/20.5 cm

YARN
Staccato Sock by Shubui (65% superwash merino/ 30% silk/5% nylon; 191 yd/176 m; 50 grams): Ivory #101, 2 hanks or substitute any sock-weight (#1) superwash wool blend

NEEDLES
1 set US 2/2.75 mm double-pointed needles (or size needed to obtain gauge)

NOTIONS
Stitch holder

Yarn needle

GAUGE
30 stitches and 39 rows per 4 in/10 cm in stockinette stitch

Instructions (make 2)

lacy cuff

CO 60 sts on 3 dpns. Join, taking care not to twist. Work lacy cuff chart, Rows 1–8:

Rnd 1: *Yo, k1, yo, k2, [k2tog] twice, k2, yo, k2tog, k1; rep from * around.

Rnd 2 (and all even rnds through rnd 8): Knit.

Rnd 3: *Yo, k3, yo, k1, [k2tog] twice, k1, yo, k2tog, k1; rep from * around.

Rnd 5: *Yo, k5, yo, [k2tog] twice, yo, k2tog, k1; rep from * around.

Rnd 7: *Yo, k3, k2tog, k2, [yo, k2tog] twice, k1; rep from * around.

Rnd 9: Knit, decreasing 4 sts evenly around—56 sts.

Rnds 10–13: *K2, p2; rep from * around.

heel flap

Place 28 sts on one needle. Place rem instep sts on stitch holder and continue in rows as follows:

Row 1 (RS): *Sl 1, k1; rep from * across.

Row 2: Sl 1, purl to end.

Rep rows 1 and 2 for 17 more times, or until heel flap is square.

heel turn

Row 1: (RS) Sl 1, k15, ssk, k1, turn.

Row 2: Sl 1, p6, p2tog, p1, turn.

Row 3: Sl 1, k7, ssk, k1, turn.

Row 4: Sl 1, p8, p2tog, p1, turn.

Continue in this manner, slipping first st, working to 1 st before gap, and working sts before and after gap tog, until all heel sts are worked (18 sts rem).

CONTINUED

	人	O	人	O			人			O	7
	人	O	人	人	O					O	5
	人	O		人	人		O			O	3
	人	O			人	人		O		O	1

STITCH KEY

☉	Yarn over
☐	Knit
人	K2tog

gusset

Setup rnd: Needle 1: Knit heel sts, pick up and knit 16 sts along side
   of heel flap; Needle 2: Knit 28 instep sts; Needle 3: Pick up and knit
   16 sts along side of heel flap, then knit first 9 sts of heel from Needle 1.
   Rounds beg and end at this point—78 sts.
Rnd 1: Needle 1: Knit to 3 sts before the end of needle, k2tog, k1;
   Needle 2: Knit across instep sts; Needle 3: K1, ssk, knit to end of rnd.
Rnd 2: Knit 1 rnd even.
Rep rnds 1 and 2 until 56 sts rem.

foot

Work even in St st until foot measures 8 in/20.5 cm from back of heel.

toe

Rnd 1: Needle 1: Knit to last 3 sts, k2tog, k1; Needle 2: K1, ssk, knit
   to last 3 sts, k2tog, k1; Needle 3: K1, ssk, knit to end of rnd.
Rnd 2: Knit 1 rnd even.
Rep rnds 1 and 2 until 20 sts rem.

finishing

Place rem sts evenly on 2 dpns. Using a yarn needle and the yarn tail,
   sew the toe closed using the Kitchener stitch.

WILD WARMERS

LITTLE ZEBRA LEG COZIES

....

If you like bold graphic prints, then intarsia will be your new KFF (knitting friend forever). You can easily chart any basic design into your knitting. All it takes is a little patience and creativity. This project takes a zebra print and turns it into simple blocks of color for eye-catching baby leggings that will have you wild for intarsia.

Instructions (make 2)

tip: To prevent holes, twist the working ends of yarn when switching colors.

Using MC, CO 36 sts.
Rows 1–6: *K2, p2; rep from * to end.
Rows 7–34: Using MC and CC, work intarsia chart, Rows 1–28.
  Cut CC.
Rows 35–40: Using MC only, *K2, p2; rep from * to end.
BO in rib patt, leaving tail for seaming.

finishing

Block.
With yarn needle, sew seam up back.
Weave in ends.

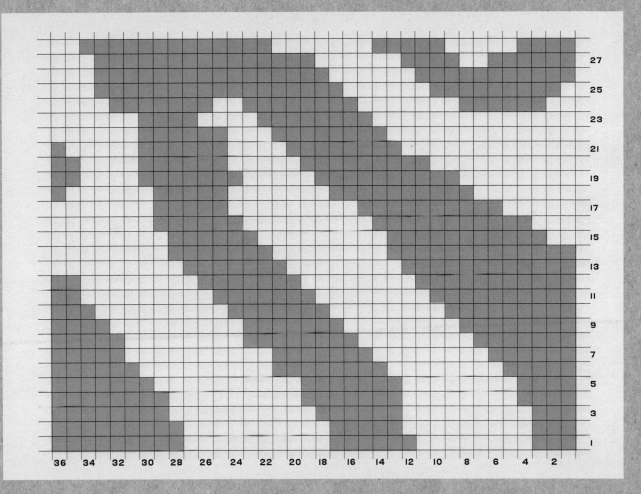

STITCH KEY

MC
CC

CADET ABOUT IT

TWISTED RIB CADET CAP

Knitting a hat from start to finish in the round is great and all, but combining different methods of construction to achieve a similar shape is extra knit-tastic. This project takes a bit more skill—but don't worry, you've totally got this! Cadet About It will give you practice seeing a piece come together in an unexpected manner. You'll start with a straight, flat piece, then pick up stitches, and join to work in the round. It's a classic hat, but with a twist!

SKILLS

Knitting in the Round with a Circular Needle (page 22)

Knitting in the Round with Double-Pointed Needles (page 23)

Twisted Rib Stitch

SIZE

Unisex (one size)

FINISHED MEASUREMENTS

Stretches to fit up to a 23-in/58-cm head

YARN

Vickie Howell Sheep(ish) for Bernat (70% acrylic/30% wool; 167 yd/153 m): Gun Metal(ish), 2 balls or substitute any worsted-weight (#4) wool blend

NEEDLES

1 set US 8/5 mm needles (optional; use circular needle for straight knitting if desired)

US 8/5 mm circular needle, 20 in/51 cm (or size needed to obtain gauge)

1 set US 8/5 mm double-pointed needles

NOTIONS

Yarn needle

Sheet of plastic canvas

GAUGE

18 stitches and 22 rows per 4 in/10 cm in k2, p2 rib

Instructions

special stitch
Right Twist (RT)
K2tog but do not slip sts off needle; insert RH needle between the 2 sts and knit the first st again; slip both sts off needle.

front

Using straight needles, CO 32 sts.
Rows 1–2: *K2, p2; rep from * to end.
Row 3: *RT, p2; rep from * to end.
Row 4: (WS) *K2, p2; rep from * to end.
These 4 rows make the twisted rib pattern.
Rep Rows 1–4 until front measures 6 in/15 cm from CO edge, ending with a WS row.
BO in patt.

back

Using straight needles, CO 98 sts.
Rows 1–2: *K2, p2; rep from * to last 2 sts, k2.
Row 3: (RS) *RT, p2; rep from * to last 2 sts, RT.
Row 4: *K2, p2; rep from * to last 2 sts, k2.
Rep Rows 1–4 until back measures 4 in/10 cm, ending with a WS row.
Slip sts onto circular needle. With RS facing, pick up 50 sts along the 6-in/15-cm edge of front piece—148 sts.
Pm; beg working twisted rib patt in rnds for 1½ in/4 cm.

crown shaping

Change to dpns when necessary.
Rnd 1: (dec rnd) *K2tog, p2; rep from * around—111 sts.
Rnd 2: *K1, p2; rep from * around.
Rnd 3: *K1, P2tog; rep from * around—74 sts.
Rnd 4: *K1, p1; rep from * around.
Rnd 5: *K2tog; rep from * around—37 sts.
Rnds 6, 8, and 10: Knit 1 rnd even.
Rnd 7: *K2tog; rep from * to last st, k1—19 sts.

CONTINUED

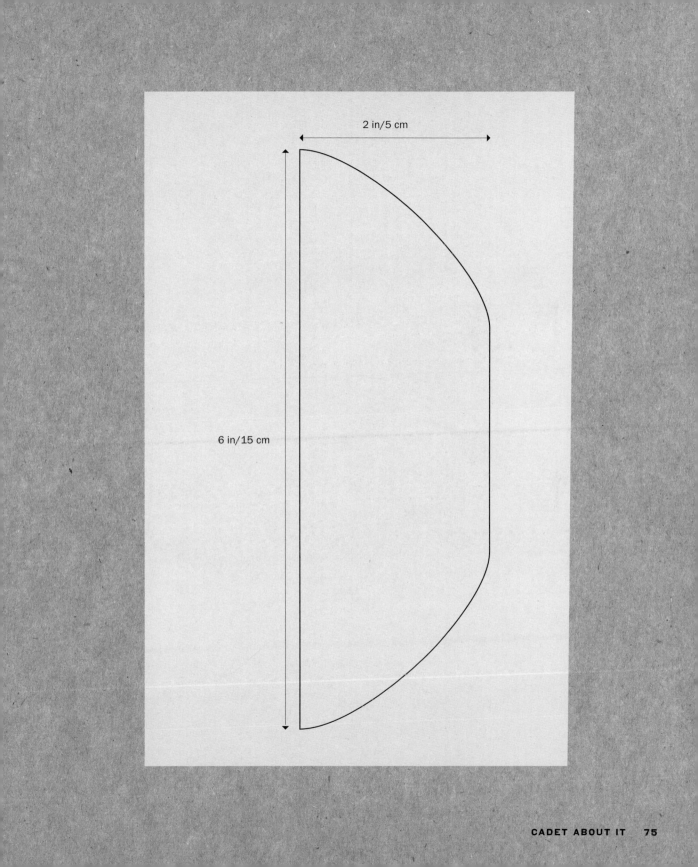

2 in/5 cm

6 in/15 cm

Rnd 9: *K2tog; rep from * to last st, k1—10 sts.

Rnd 11: *K2tog; rep from * around—5 sts.

Break yarn, leaving 10 in/25.5 cm tail. Weave tail through live stitches, letting them drop off needles; pull crown closed. Push tail through to underside and tie off.

Seam back and front side edges.

brim

Row 1: With straight needles, RS facing, pick up and knit 32 sts along lower edge of front piece.

Rows 2 and 4: (WS) Purl all sts.

Row 3: Knit all sts.

Row 5: K2tog, knit to last 2 sts, ssk.

Row 6: P2tog, purl to last 2 sts, ssp—28 sts.

Rows 7 and 8: Work 2 rows even.

Rows 9 and 10: Repeat Rows 5 and 6—24 sts.

Row 11: K2tog (twice), knit to last 4 sts, ssk (twice)—20 sts.

Row 12: P2tog (twice), purl to last 4 sts, ssp (twice)—16 sts.

Row 13: Repeat Row 11—12 sts.

Row 14: (WS, turning ridge): Knit all sts.

Row 15: [K1, inc 1] twice, knit to last 2 sts, [inc 1, K1] twice—16 sts.

Row 16: [P1, inc 1] twice, purl to last 2 sts, [inc 1, P1] twice—20 sts.

Row 17: Repeat Row 15—24 sts.

Row 18: Purl all sts.

Row 19: K1, inc 1, knit to last st, inc 1, K1—26 sts.

Row 20: P1, inc 1, purl to last st, inc 1, P1—28 sts.

Rows 21 and 22: Work even in St st.

Row 23: Repeat row 19—30 sts.

Row 24: Repeat row 20—32 sts.

Rows 25–28: Work 4 rows even in St st.

BO, leaving 12-in/30.5-cm tail for seaming.

finishing

Using template on page 75, cut out plastic canvas brim piece. Fold knitted hat brim in half at the turning ridge, creating a pocket, and place canvas piece inside. Using tail and yarn needle, seam closed.

Weave in ends.

SLOUCHER BEANIE

CABLE AND EYELET CAP

·······················

The meandering cable-and-eyelet pattern in this cap looks crazy-hard, but it isn't at all once you get into the groove. The tension of the cables juxtaposed with the open weave of the eyelet give unexpected interest to the otherwise unstructured drape of this hat. Worked in the round without any shaping, the Sloucher Beanie will show off both your awesome sense of style and your mad knitting skills!

SKILLS

Basic Cable Left (page 13)

Eyelet Stitch (page 19)

Knitting in the Round with
a Circular Needle (page 22)

Knitting in the Round with
Double-Pointed Needles
(page 23)

SIZE

Women's S/M

FINISHED
MEASUREMENTS

Circumference: 18 in/46 cm
(before stretching)

Length: 11 in/28 cm

YARN

Vickie Howell Sheep(ish)
for Bernat (70% acrylic/
30% wool) 167 yd/153 m):
Pumpkin(ish), 1 ball
or substitute any worsted-
weight (#4) wool blend

NEEDLES

US 9/5.5 mm circular needle,
16 to 20 in/40.5 to 51 cm
long (or size needed to
obtain gauge)

NOTIONS

Cable needle

Yarn needle

Markers

GAUGE

19 stitches and 25 rows per
4 in/10 cm in pattern stitch,
when slightly stretched

Instructions

Starting at ribbed edge, CO 88 sts. Join, taking care not to twist.

Rnds 1–10: *K2, p2; rep from * around.

Rnd 11: Knit, inc 2 sts evenly around—90 sts.

note: Only count stitches after Rnds 12, 25, 26, and 39.

Rnd 12: P2, *k6, p2; rep from * around.

Rnd 13: P2, [k2tog, yo] twice, k2tog, *p2, k6, p2, [k2tog, yo] twice, k2tog; rep from * to last two sts, p2.

Rnds 14, 16, 18, 20, 22, and 24: P2, k5, p2, *k6, p2, k5, p2; rep from * to last 7 sts, k5, p2.

Rnds 15 and 23: P2, k1, [yo, k2tog] twice, p2, *6-st LC, p2, k1, [yo, k2tog] twice, p2; rep from * around.

Rnds 17, 19, and 21: P2, k1, [yo, k2tog] twice, p2, *k6, p2, k1, [yo, k2tog] twice, p2; rep from * around.

Rnd 25: P2, k2, yo, k1, yo, k2tog, p2, *k6, p2, k2, yo, k1, yo, k2tog, p2; rep from * around.

Rnd 26: Repeat Rnd 12.

Rnd 27: P2, k6, p2, *yb, sl 1, k1, psso, [yo, sl 1, k1, psso] twice, p2, k6, p2; rep from * around.

Rnds 28, 30, 32, 34, 36, and 38: P2, k6, p2, *k5, p2, k6, p2; rep from * around.

Rnds 29 and 37: P2, 6-st LC, p2, *yb, [sl 1, k1, psso, yo] twice, k1, p2, 6-st LC, p2; rep from * around.

Rnd 31, 33, and 35: P2, k6, p2, *yb, [sl 1, k1, psso, yo] twice, k1, p2, k6, p2; rep from * around.

Rnd 39: K6, p2, *k2, yo sl 1, k1, psso, yo, k1, p2, k6, p2; rep from * around.

Repeat Rnds 12–39 until piece measures 11 in/28 cm from CO edge. BO.

finishing

For seaming and closing the hat, thread the tail through a yarn needle, insert into top center, and sew a couple of sts. Pinch side edges to the same center point and stitch the edges together. The top of the hat will now be in a star formation. Continue to pinch opposite edges and stitch them together until top of the hat is completely closed. Fasten off. For a step-by-step tutorial on seaming a hat, go to my YouTube page for a video.

Using yarn needle, weave in ends

DOWNWARD SPIRAL

SPIRAL TOP BEANIE

....

You can never have too many ribbed beanies. Especially if they are creatively knitted. You can easily rise above fashion Snoresville with just a Downward Spiral—a beanie with plain old decreases, spaced apart, creating a pinwheel effect at the crown!

SKILLS
Spiral Decreasing
Knitting in the Round with a
Circular Needle (page 22)
Knitting in the Round with
Double-Pointed Needles
(page 23)

SIZES
Child's (Women's, Men's)

FINISHED MEASUREMENTS
Circumference: Stretches to fit
20(22, 23) in/51(56, 58) cm

YARN
Lorna's Laces Sport
(100% superwash wool;
200 yd/217 m): Pullman,
2 hanks or substitute any sport-
weight (#2) superwash wool

NEEDLES
US 6/4 mm circular needle,
18 in/46 cm long

1 set US 6/4 mm
double-pointed needles (or size
needed to obtain gauge)

NOTIONS
Yarn needle

GAUGE
24 stitches and 28 rows per
4 in/10 cm in k2, p2 rib,
slightly stretched

Instructions

body

Using circ, CO 100(120, 130) sts. Join, taking care not to twist.
Work in k2, p2 rib until piece measures 5½(6, 6½) in/14(15, 16.5) cm.

decreasing for crown

Change to dpns when necessary.
Rnd 1: *K8, k2tog; rep from * around.
Rnd 2 and all even-numbered rounds: Knit 1 rnd even.
Rnd 3: *K7, k2tog; rep from * around.
Rnd 5: *K6, k2tog; rep from * around.
Rnd 7: *K5, k2tog; rep from * around.
Rnd 9: *K4, k2tog; rep from * around.
Rnd 11: *K3, k2tog; rep from * around.
Rnd 13: *K2, k2tog; rep from * around.
Rnd 15: *K1, k2tog; rep from * around.
Rnd 17: *K2tog; rep from * around—10(12, 13) sts.
Cut yarn, leaving a 12-in/30.5-cm tail.

finishing

Using yarn needle, thread tail through remaining sts. Pull snugly
to close.
Weave in ends.

SQUARED UP

TODDLER'S MITERED SQUARE BEANIE

....

When you think about making a beanie, squares probably aren't the first things that come to mind. But just like with Cadet About It (page 73), this project will help you think of innovative ways to create a traditional shape. Squared Up pieces together mitered squares to create the "ring" that makes up the body of a beanie. Sometimes, it's hip to be square!

Instructions

note: This beanie is made by joining squares to make the body, then picking up stitches for the crown and band. Color not in use may be carried loosely up the side to avoid having multiple ends to weave in.

body

mitered squares
Make 15(17) striped and 1 solid in color of choice (CC shown on sample.) With CC and 2 dpns, CO 18 sts; pm between 2 center sts (sts 9 and 10).

Row 1: (RS) K to 2 sts before marker, k2tog tbl, sl marker, k2tog, k to end.

Row 2: Knit 1 row even.

Join MC.

Repeat Rows 1 and 2.

Cont as est, repeating 2-row stripes, until 2 sts remain.

BO last 2 sts on WS row.

square edging
Using crochet hook and MC, work 1 row of sc evenly around each square, taking care to work 3 sc at all corners to prevent bunching. Fasten off.

assembling squares
Lay squares in 2 rows, one above the other, in desired pattern.

With RS together, join squares by whip stitching through back loops of crocheted sts. You are working on the horizontal seam between the 2 strips of attached mitered squares.

Seam squares together along vertical sides.

With RS together, join first 2 squares to the last 2 to form circular hat body.

band
With RS facing, and using the circ and MC, pick up 64(72) sts evenly spaced around lower edge of mitered square body. Join.

Work in k2, p2 rib for 6 rounds.

BO in k2, p2 rib.

crown

With RS facing, using the circ and CC, pick up 64(70) sts evenly spaced
around top edge of mitered square ring. Join.

note: Change to dpns when necessary.

Rnds 1–5, 7, 9, and 11: Knit.
Rnd 6: *K2tog, k1; rep from * to last st, k1—43(47) sts.
Rnd 8: *K2tog; repeat from * to last st, k1—22(24) sts.
Rnd 10: *K2tog; repeat from * around—11(12) sts rem.
Cut yarn, leaving a long tail. Thread tail through stitches of last round.
Pull snugly to close opening. Fasten off end.

finishing

Using yarn needle, weave in all ends.

HEAD SPACE

LACY HEADBAND

Eyelet lace is the gateway stitch to more complex lace stitches. It beautifully creates a nice open-weave fabric, but is easy enough that you can watch TV while knitting it. Head Space will get you into the lacy groove without taking too much time, and is the perfect accessory for tossing back your hair on the go!

SKILLS
Eyelet Stitch (page 19)

SIZE
One size

FINISHED
MEASUREMENTS
Knitted portion: 2½ in/6 cm
wide by 14 in/35.5 cm long

YARN
Madeline Tosh Merino Lite
(100% superwash merino
wool; 420 yd/384 m):
Espadrilles, 1 hank (1 hank
will make many headbands)
or substitute any fingering-
weight (#1) superwash wool

NEEDLES
US 3/3.25 mm needles (or
size needed to obtain gauge)

NOTIONS
20-in/50-cm piece of thin
cording or elastic

Yarn needle

Sewing needle

Thread

GAUGE
24 stitches and 18 rows per
4 in/10 cm in pattern stitch

Instructions

CO 12 sts.
Rows 1–30: Knit.
Row 31: (RS) [Kf&b] 3 times, k across to last 3 sts, [kf&b] 3 times—
    18 sts.
Row 32: Knit.
Row 33: K3, *k2tog, yo; rep from * to last 3 sts, k3.
Row 34: K2, purl to last 2 sts, k2.
Row 35: K5, *k2tog, yo; rep from * until last 5 sts, k5.
Row 36: Rep Row 34.
Rep Rows 33–36, until piece measures 11 in/28 cm from CO edge.
Next Row: (RS) Ssk 3 times, k to last 6 sts, k2tog 3 times—12 sts rem.
Rep Rows 1–30.
BO.

finishing

Block.
Make a loop out of cording by folding the piece and tying or hand-sewing
    the ends together. Using a yarn needle and yarn, fold the headband
    end over cording (creates a casing for it) and sew seam closed.
Repeat for opposite end.

CABLE ACE

ETERNITY SCARF

....

Once you get the hang of knitting basic cables (see pages 13 and 14), moving on to more complex cables isn't difficult. Often, it's just a matter of applying the same concept, but multiple times or at varying intervals, as is the case with this Eternity Scarf. The intricate design will impress your knitty friends while upping the ante of your cable knitting skills. You'll be hooked on cables by the time you finish the project.

Instructions

special stitch

8-stitch Left Purl Cable (8-st LPC)
Sl 3 sts to cn and hold to front, k3, p2, then k3 from cn.

> **note:** To double-strand yarn without using two balls at a time, pull one end from the center and one from the outside of the same ball.

With double-strand yarn, CO 40 sts.
Rows 1, 3, 19, 21, 23, 25, and 27: [K2, p2] twice, p3; work cable chart across next 18 sts as follows: [k3, p2] 3 times, k3; end p3, [p2, k2] twice.
Row 2 and all WS rows: [P2, k2] twice, k3; p3, [k2, p3] 3 times; k3, [p2, k2] twice.
Rows 5, 9, 13, and 17: [K2, p2] twice, p3; k3, p2, 8-st LPC, p2, k3; p3, [p2, k2] twice.
Rows 7, 11, and 15: [K2, p2] twice, p3; 8-st LPC, p2, 8-st LPC; p3, [p2, k2] twice.
Row 28: [P2, k2] twice, k3; p3, [k2, p3] 3 times; k3, [p2, k2] twice.
Repeat Rows 1–28 a total of 7 times.

finishing

If necessary, block.
Sew CO and BO edges together to create loop.
Weave in ends.

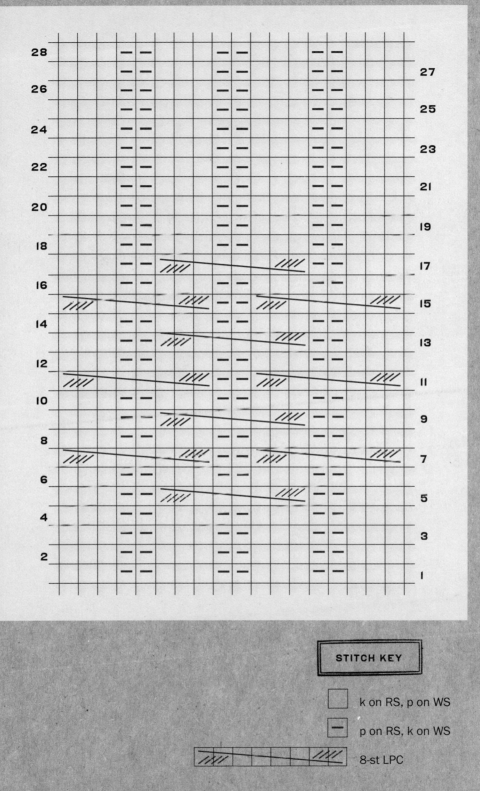

STITCH KEY

☐ k on RS, p on WS

— p on RS, k on WS

8-st LPC

FAIR WEATHER

FAIR ISLE PONCHETTE

....

Fair Isle is a popular way to work with color while knitting. While this technique is often associated with a more delicate and conservative style, you can make it modern by using a heavier yarn and bigger patterns. Applied to a nontraditional accessory like a shoulder cowl, and it's a whole new knitting world, people! Fair Isle can be as simple or complex as you'd like, but the result is always a nice, graphic look. Fair Weather starts you off easy; from here, the opportunities are endless for your Fair Isle Ponchette adventure!

SKILLS
Two-Color Fair Isle
Knitting in the Round with
a Circular Needle (page 22)

SIZE
Women's S/M(L/XL)

MEASUREMENTS
Circumference (widest point):
39(45) in/99(114.5) cm

Length: 17 in/43 cm

YARN
Vickie Howell Sheep(ish)
for Bernat (70% acrylic/
30% wool; 167 yd/153 m):
(A) Taupe(ish) and (C) Teal(ish),
2 balls each; (B) Plum(ish),
1 ball or substitute any worsted-
weight (#4) wool blend

NEEDLES
US 6/4 mm circular needle,
24 in/61 cm long (or size
needed to obtain gauge)

US 7/4.5 mm circular needle,
24 in/61 cm long (or size
larger than the smaller needle)

1 set US 6/4 mm
double-pointed needles

NOTIONS
Yarn needle

Length of faux suede cord

GAUGE
20 stitches by 23 rows per
4 in/10 cm in St st using
smaller needles

Instructions

Starting at the bottom edge, using larger needles and Color A,
CO 196(224) sts. Join in rnd, taking care not to twist.

Rnds 1–2: With Color A, work in garter stitch (in the round, this means knit 1 rnd, purl 1 rnd).

Rnds 3–4: With Color C, work in garter stitch.

Rnds 5–42: Rep Rnds 1–4.

Optional for longer cowl, work more rnds in this manner.

Switch to smaller circ needle.

Rnds 43–47: With Color A, knit.

Rnds 48–49: With Color B, knit.

Rnds 50–51: With Color A, knit.

Rnds 52–62: Using Colors A and C, follow chart Rows 1–11.

Rnds 63–71: With Color A, knit.

note: Switch to dpns as necessary.

Rnd 72: With Color A knit, while dec 38 sts evenly around—
158(186) sts rem.

Rnds 73–74: Knit.

Rnd 75: Rep Rnd 72—120(148) sts rem.

Rnds 76–77: Knit.

Rnd 78 (eyelet rnd): *K4, yo, k2tog; rep from * around.

Rnd 79: Knit.

Rnds 80 and 82: With Color C, *k2, p2; rep from * around.

Rnds 81 and 83: With Color A, *k2, p2; rep from * around.

Rep Rnds 80–83 until rib section measures 6 in/15 cm. Cut Color C.
Join Color B.

Cont in k2, p2 rib, with Color B, work 1 rnd. Cut Color B. Join Color A.

With Color A, BO in rib.

tip: When a pattern doesn't specify which type of decrease method to use, assume that you can choose your favorite method. I tend to use k2tog the most.

finishing

Weave in ends.

Block.

Weave cord through eyelet holes; tie in bow.

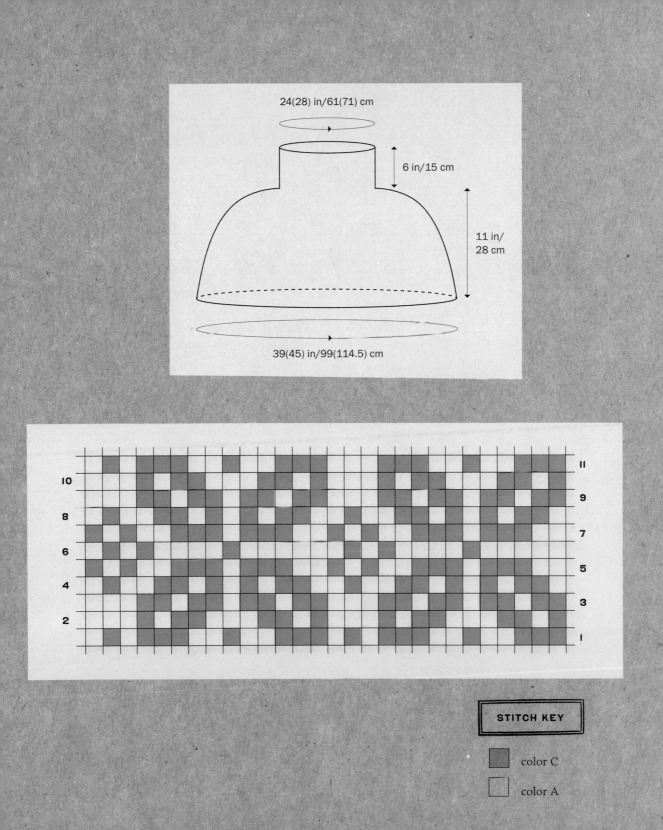

24(28) in/61(71) cm

6 in/15 cm

11 in/
28 cm

39(45) in/99(114.5) cm

11
10
9
8
7
6
5
4
3
2
1

STITCH KEY

color C

color A

BRIOCHE THE SUBJECT

DOUBLE-SIDED RIB SCARF

....

The brioche stitch creates a lush-looking, thick fabric. When worked in a two-color variation like in Brioche the Subject, you get the added "shadow" effect with a different color predominant on either side. I'll be honest: this technique can be a little persnickety. Each row of the two-row pattern is essentially worked twice, alternating between working sets of slipped stitches and yarn-overs, then working the pairs together to create the double-sided pattern. Once you get the hang of it though, you'll feel like a pro and have a super-cool scarf to show off!

SKILLS
Brioche Stitch (pages 16–17)
Brioche Bind-Off
Adding Fringe

SIZE
Unisex (one size)

**FINISHED
MEASUREMENTS**
Width: 5 in/12.5 cm
(slightly stretched)
Length: 60 in/152 cm
(without fringe)

YARN
Vickie Howell Sheep(ish)
for Bernat (70% acrylic/
30% wool; 167 yd/153 m):
(CC) Gray(ish) and (MC) Gun
Metal(ish), 1 ball each
or substitute any worsted-
weight (#4) wool blend

NEEDLES
US 8/5 mm circular needle,
any length (or size needed to
obtain gauge)

NOTIONS
Crochet hook (any size)
Yarn needle

GAUGE
14 stitches and 16 rows per
4 in/10 cm in pattern stitch

Instructions

With MC, CO 18 sts. Do not turn work.

Prep Row: (RS CC, forms purl columns in CC on RS) Slide work to other tip of needle and attach CC; wyif, *sl 1, yo, p1; rep from * across. Turn work.

Row 1: (WS MC, forms purl columns in MC) Wyif, *sl 1, yo, bp1 (purl together the slipped stitch and yo from row before); rep from *across. Do not turn; slide sts to opposite end of needle where CC is attached.

Row 1: (WS CC, forms knit columns in CC) With CC, *bk1 (knit together the slipped stitch and yo from row before), yf, sl 1, yo; rep from * across. Turn work.

Row 2: (RS MC, forms knit columns in MC) Maintain the CC yo of last worked st by holding it under left needle to the back; with MC, *bk1, yf, sl 1, yo; rep from * across. Do not turn; slide sts to opposite end of needle where CC is attached.

Row 2: (RS CC, forms purl columns in CC) With CC, wyif, *sl 1, yo, bp1; rep from * across. Turn work.

Repeat Rows 1 and 2 RS and WS with colors indicated, until scarf measures 60 in/152 cm and finishing with a RS CC row.

BO using CC as follows: K1, bp1, pass second st over first st on the RH needle (one st bound off). Cont in this manner, knitting the knit sts and bp1 (the sl st and yo) while binding off.

Cut both colors, leaving 6 in/15 cm tails.

finishing

fringe (make 12)

Using MC, cut 5 strands of yarn *double* the length that you'd like your finished fringe to be. Holding strands together, fold in half. Insert a crochet hook (any size) through the right side of the edge of your project and lay yarn at folded point over the hook. Pull the yarn through, from back to front, just enough to create a loop. Set aside crochet hook and use your hands to fold loop over edge of project and pull ends of yarn through loop. Pull until taught. Repeat this process, attaching 6 fringe bunches evenly across each scarf end.

Weave in ends.

Block if necessary.

STOP, DROP, AND CABLE

DROPPED-STITCH CABLED COWL

·····················

The combination of dropped stitches and cables in this project gives the look of twisted columns and ladders. This funky take on a cowl shows you how a cable can stop a dropped stitch in its tracks, while leaving "runs" in the knitted fabric. Knit this cowl and your skill level will be on fire. You know what to do: Stop, drop, and cable!

SIZE
Unisex (one size)

**FINISHED
MEASUREMENTS**
Circumference: 11½ in/29 cm
Length: 21 in/53 cm

YARN
Vickie Howell Sheep(ish)
for Bernat (70% acrylic/
30% wool: 167 yd/153 m):
Magenta(ish), 1 ball
or substitute any worsted-
weight (#4) wool blend

NEEDLES
US 9/5.5 mm circular needle,
16 in/40.5 cm long (or size
needed to obtain gauge)

NOTIONS
Cable needle
Marker
Yarn needle

GAUGE
14 stitches and 17 rows per
4 in/10 cm in stockinette stitch

Instructions

CO 84 sts. Join, taking care not to twist.
Work in k3, p3 ribbing for 1½ in/4 cm.
Setup Rnd: Knit, increasing 4 sts evenly around—88 sts.
Begin 21-row dropped-stitch cable chart:
Rnd 1: *K2, work [6-st RC] 3 times, k2; rep from * around.
Rnds 2–10: Knit.
Rnd 11: *4-st RC, [k2, 4-st RC] 3 times; rep from * around.
Rnds 12–20: Knit.
Rnd 21: *K2, [sl 2 sts onto cn and hold in front, drop 2 sts, k2, k2 from cn] 3 times, k2; rep from * around.
Rnd 22: Knit.
Rnd 23: *K2, [k2, M1, k1, M1, k1] 3 times, k2; rep from * around.
Rnd 24: Knit.
Rep chart Rnds 1–21, and Rnds 22–24 one more time.
Next rnd: Knit, dec 4 sts evenly around—84 sts rem.
Work k3, p3 ribbing for 1½ in/4 cm.
BO in ribbing.

finishing

Weave in yarn ends.
Gently pull on sides of dropped stitches to form spaces.

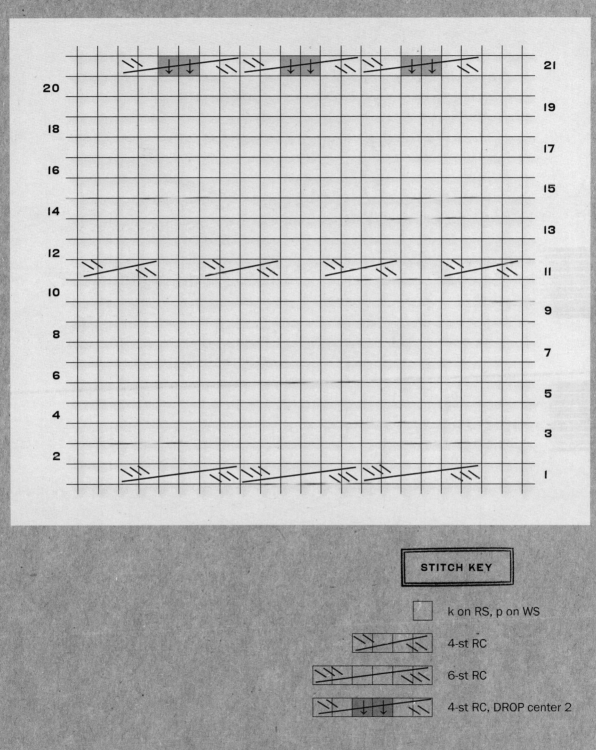

STITCH KEY

□ k on RS, p on WS

4-st RC

6-st RC

4-st RC, DROP center 2

RAINDROP WRAP

TRIANGLE LACE SHAWL

....

Knitting triangle lace shawls can be intimidating—at least it was for me when I started out. But it doesn't have to be. A simple repeat guided by charts and paired with a gorgeous, hand-dyed yarn leads to a show-stopping yet totally attainable project! The Raindrop Wrap is knit from the top-center out and has a droplet-inspired motif, which will take your skills to the next level and make you look like a master.

SKILLS
Lace Knitting
Reading Triangle Lace Charts
(page 114)
Blocking (page 14)

SIZE
Women's (one size)

FINISHED MEASUREMENTS
Triangle shape: 70 in/178 cm
by 35 in/89 cm

YARN
Madeline Tosh Merino Lite
(100% superwash merino
wool; 420 yd/384 m):
Curiosity, 1 hank
or substitute any fingering-
weight (#1) merino wool

NEEDLES
US 7/4.5 mm needles (or size
needed to obtain gauge)

NOTIONS
Markers
Yarn needle

GAUGE
16 stitches per approx.
4 in/10 cm in garter stitch
(blocked)

Instructions

To begin point of wrap, CO 5 sts.
Rows 1–2: Knit.
Row 3: K1, kf&b, k1, kf&b, k1—7 sts.
Row 4: Knit.

Work Chart 1 as follows:

tip: Place a stitch marker at the center stitch and at every pattern repeat to help you keep count.

Row 1: K2 (border sts), [yo, k1, yo] (repeat from chart), pm, k1 (center st), pm, [yo, k1, yo] (repeat), k2 (border sts, not shown on chart)—11 sts.
Row 2, and all WS rows: Knit or purl as indicated on chart.
Row 3: K2, *yo, k2tog, yo, k1, yo*, k1; rep ** once more, k2—15 sts.
Row 5: K2, *yo, k1, k2tog, yo, k2, yo*, k1; rep ** once more, k2—19 sts.
Row 7: K2, *yo, k1, k2tog, yo, ktbl, yo, skp, k1, yo*, k1; rep from ** once more, k2—23 sts.
Row 9: K2, *yo, k1, k2tog, yo, k3, yo, skp, k1, yo*, k1; rep ** once more, k2—27 sts.
Row 11: K2, *yo, k2, skp, yo, k3, yo, k2tog, k2, yo*, k1; rep ** once more, k2—31 sts.

Work Chart 2 as follows:
Row 1: K2, *yo, k2tog, yo, k2, skp, yo, ktbl, yo, k2tog, k1, k2tog, yo, k1, yo*, k1; rep ** once more, k2—35 sts.
Row 2, and all WS rows: Knit or purl as indicated on chart.
Row 3: K2, *yo, k1, k2tog, yo, k8, k2tog, yo, k2, yo*, k1; rep ** once more, k2.
Row 5: K2, *yo, k1, k2tog, yo, ktbl, yo, skp, k5, k2tog, yo*, ktbl, yo, skp, k1, yo*, k1; rep ** once more, k2.
Row 7: K2, *yo, k1, k2tog, yo, k3, yo, skp, k3, k2tog, yo, k3, yo, skp, k1, yo*, k1; rep ** once more, k2.
Row 9: K2, *yo, k2, skp, yo, k3, yo, k2tog, k3, k2tog, yo, k3, yo, k2tog, k2, yo*, k1; rep ** once more, k2.
Row 11: K2, *yo, k2tog, yo, k2, skp, yo, ktbl, yo, k2tog, k1, k2tog, yo, k2, skp, yo, ktbl, yo, k2tog, k1, k2tog, yo, k1, yo*, k1; rep ** once more, k2.
Row 13: K2, *yo, k1, k2tog, [yo, k8, k2tog] twice, yo, k2, yo*, k1; rep ** once more, k2.

Row 15: K2, *yo, k1, [k2tog, yo, ktbl, yo, skp, k5] twice, k2tog, yo, ktbl, yo, skp, k1, yo*, k1; rep ** once more, k2.

Row 17: K2, *yo, k1, [K2tog, yo, k3, yo, skp, k3] twice, k2tog, yo, k3, yo, skp, k1, yo*, k1; rep ** once more, k2.

Row 19: K2, *yo, [k2, skp, yo, k3, yo, k2tog, k1] 3 times, k1, yo*, k1; rep ** once more, k2.

Continue as est, keeping a 2-st border at each end, a center st, and the 10-st repeat as necessary to continue to expand your wrap until it measures 33 in/84 cm (approx 30 patt repeats) from CO edge.

edging

Work Chart 3 as follows:

Row 1: K2 (edge sts), yo, k2, *k3, skp, yo, ktbl, yo, k2tog, k2*; rep ** until 3 sts before center st. K3, yo, k1 (center st), yo, k2; rep ** until 5 sts before end. K3, yo, k2 (edge sts).

Row 2 (and all WS rows): Knit or purl as indicated on chart.

Row 3: K2 (edge sts), yo, k2, yo, *k1, yo, k7, yo*; rep ** until 3 sts before center st. K1, yo, k2, yo, k1 (center st), yo, k2, yo; rep ** until 5 sts before end. K1, yo, k2, yo, k2 (edge sts).

Row 5: K2 (edge sts), yo, k4, yo, *k1, yo, k3, s2kp, k3, yo*; rep ** until 5 sts before center st. K1, yo, k4, yo, k1 (center st), yo, k4, yo; rep ** until 7 sts before end. K1, yo, k4, yo, k2 (edge sts).

Row 7: K2 (edge sts), yo, k6, yo, *k1, yo, k3, s2kp, k3, yo*; rep ** until 7 sts before center st. K1, yo, k6, yo, k1 (center st), yo, k6, yo; rep ** until 9 sts before end. K1, yo, k6, yo, k2 (edge sts).

Row 9: K2 (edge sts), yo, k8, yo, *k1, yo, k3, s2kp, k3, yo*; rep ** until 9 sts before center st. K1, yo, k8, yo, k1 (center st), yo, k8, yo; rep ** until 11 sts before end. K1, yo, k8, yo, k2 (edge sts).

BO as follows: K1, *k1, transfer 2 sts back to LH needle and k2tog tbl; rep from * to end.

finishing

Weave in ends.
Block carefully.

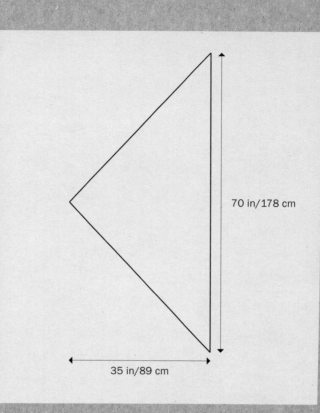

70 in/178 cm

35 in/89 cm

reading triangle lace charts

Lace shawls like the Raindrop Wrap are essentially two triangles knit simultaneously. If space allows, publishers will sometimes print a mind-blowing chart of every stitch of the piece. More often, though, the chart is broken up to representative pieces of the individual elements (beginning, overall repeat, edging, and so on). The charts will indicate the repeats for one triangle, which will be repeated (minus the center stitch) for the second. Even though the chart is oriented horizontally, the lace motif in knitted form will end up at a 45-degree angle from the center increase line. Trust me; it's magic before your eyes!

CHART 1: BEGINNING

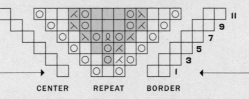

CENTER   REPEAT   BORDER

Even, a.k.a. nonpublic (wrong side), rows are often left out in lace charts to save space. You should assume that these rows are worked straight, without any pattern stitches, unless otherwise indicated.

These two border stitches will be repeated at both ends of every row for the entire body of the wrap.

CHART 2: LACE REPEAT

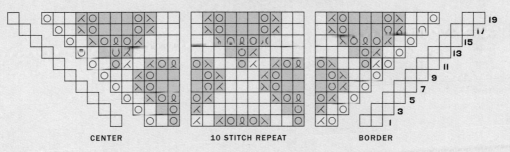

CENTER   10 STITCH REPEAT   BORDER

CHART 3: EDGING

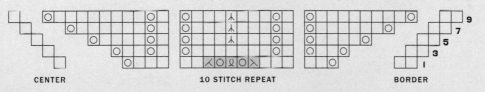

CENTER   10 STITCH REPEAT   BORDER

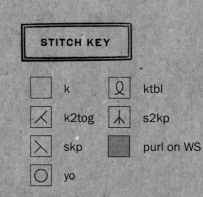

STITCH KEY

☐	k	℧	ktbl
↗	k2tog	人	s2kp
↖	skp	▓	purl on WS
○	yo		

CAPE DEAR

KID'S CAPELET

·······················

If you have a toddler in your life, chances are you're one busy knitter. Who has time to wrestle her into sleeves? That, my friend, is what capelets are for! Throw this cape over little miss's shoulders, then pat yourself on the back for finishing this project up with a fancy, picot bind-off!

Instructions

Starting on the bottom edge, CO 72(76, 80) sts.
Row 1: P2, *yo, p4tog; rep from * to last 2 sts, p2.

note: Don't count sts after first row.

Row 2: K3, [k1, p1, k1] all into the next st, *k1, [k1, p1, k1] into next st;
rep from * to last 2 sts, k2.
Row 3: Knit.
Repeat these 3 rows until piece measures 10½(12, 12½) in/
26(30.5, 31) cm, ending with a WS row.

shoulder shaping
Discontinue stitch pattern; begin working in garter stitch:
Row 1: (RS) K16(17, 18), ssk, pm, k2tog, k32(34, 36), ssk, pm, k2tog,
knit to end—4 sts decreased.
Row 2: Knit 1 row even.
Row 3: *Knit to 2 sts before marker, ssk, sl marker, k2tog; rep from
* once more, knit to end.
Rep last 2 rows 7(7, 8) more times, then Row 2 once more—
36(40, 40) sts rem.
Eyelet row: (RS) *K2, yo, k2tog; rep from * to end.
Knit 2 rows even.
BO, using Picot Bind-Off.

finishing

Weave in ends. Block if necessary.
Crochet a chain to desired length, leaving a 6-in/15-cm tail on each end
when you fasten off.
Weave chain tie through eyelet row at the neckline. Slide a bead on each
end of the tie, and knot in place.

tip: When working with bulkier or heavier yarns, do yourself a favor
and use a circular needle instead of straight needles. Although you'll
still work back and forth like you would with straights, the cords on the
circular needle will help hold the weight of the knitted fabric on your
lap so that your wrists won't have to carry it all.

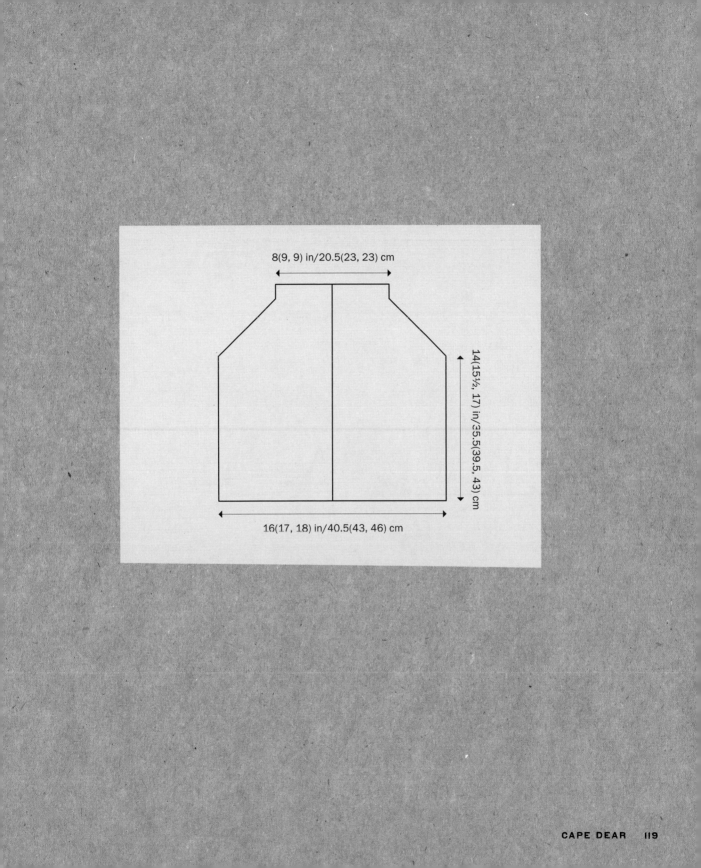

8(9, 9) in/20.5(23, 23) cm

14(15½, 17) in/35.5(39.5, 43) cm

16(17, 18) in/40.5(43, 46) cm

HOODWINKED

COZY HOODED SHRUG

....

Knitting from the top down is one of those intermediate skills that will make your garment knitting so much easier! This technique eliminates having to seam pieces together by allowing you to make your entire piece all in one. With Hoodwinked, I walk you through this technique. The result is a handy, buttoned-on shrug perfect for those chilly nights at the beach.

Instructions

body

With circ and working from the top down, CO 7(8, 9) for sleeve, pm, CO
18(22, 26) for back, pm, CO 7 (8, 9) for sleeve—32(38, 44) sts.

Do not join; work St st back and forth in rows.

Increase Row: (RS) Kf&b, knit to last st before first marker, kf&b, slip
marker, kf&b, knit to last st before second marker, kf&b, slip marker,
kf&b, knit to last st, kf&b—38(44, 50) sts.

Work 1 row even.

Cont in St st, rep last 2 rows a total of 16(16, 17) times, end after a WS
row—134(140, 146) sts.

Dividing Row: (RS) Place 39(40, 42) sleeve sts on waste yarn, BO 5(5, 7)
underarm sts, k40(44, 48) back sts, BO 5(5,7) underarm sts, place
next 39(40, 42) sleeve sts on waste yarn.

Next rows: (WS) Work even in St st on back sts only for 5 rows.

BO.

sleeve

Place 39(40, 42) held sleeve sts on dpns; pick up and knit 5(4, 6) sts for
underarm from body underarm sts. Join rnd—44(44, 48) sts.

Work in k2, p2 rib until piece measures 19(19, 19½) in/48(48, 49.5) cm
from underarm.

BO in rib.

Repeat for second sleeve.

edging

With RS facing and using circ, beg at left underarm, pick up and knit
144(152, 160) stitches as follows: 12 sts across underarm and down
side of back, 40(44, 48) sts across lower edge of back, 12 sts up side
of back and across other underarm, 25 sts up right front, 30(34, 38)
sts across back neck, 25 sts down left front. Join; pm for beg of rnd.

Work in k2, p2 rib for 1½ in/4 cm.

BO in rib.

hood

CO 56(60, 64) sts.

Work 2 rows in k2, p2 rib, end with a WS row.

Buttonhole Row: (RS) Work 12(14, 16) sts in rib, *[k2tog, yo] for buttonhole, p2; rep from * 7 more times, work to end in rib—8 buttonholes

Work 3 rows even in rib, working yo in patt on next row, end after
WS row.

Discontinue k2, p2 rib.

Change to St st, keeping first and last 4 sts in garter st for border sts
as follows:

(RS) Knit.

(WS) K4, purl to last 4 sts, k4.

Repeat last 2 rows until piece measures 13(14, 14½) in/33(35.5,
37) cm from CO edge.

Fold hood in half so that 28(30, 32) stitches are at each end of circ.
Using one of the dpns, join, using 3 needle bind-off.

finishing

Hand-sew 8 buttons across back neck band to correspond with hood
buttonholes.

Weave in ends.

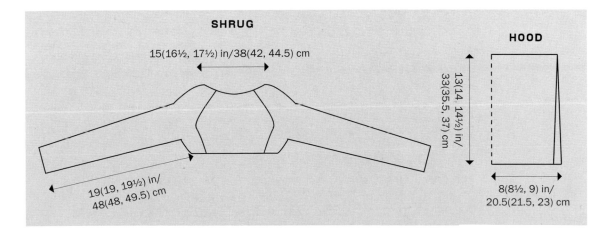

SHRUG

15(16½, 17½) in/38(42, 44.5) cm

HOOD

13(14, 14½) in/
33(35.5, 37) cm

19(19, 19½) in/
48(48, 49.5) cm

8(8½, 9) in/
20.5(21.5, 23) cm

VESTED INTEREST

SPARKLY VEST

....

A shimmery little vest is great for layering, and works for almost any occasion. A vest is also the perfect gateway project to knitting a full sweater (you know, when you're ready to make the sleeve commitment). Vested Interest combines a simple, textured, half-linen stitch with a touch of razzle-dazzle. Knit now; sparkle later!

Instructions

back

Cast on 65(71, 79, 87) sts.
Setup Row: Purl.
Row 1: (RS) K1 (selvage st), *k1, yf, sl next st purlwise, yb; repeat from * to last 2 sts, k1, k1 (selvage st).

note: First and last sts of all rows count as selvage sts.

Row 2: Purl.
Row 3: K3, *yf, sl 1 st, yb, k1; repeat from * to last 2 sts, k2.
Row 4: Purl.
Repeating these 4 rows makes patt st.
Work in patt st until piece measures 2½ in/6 cm from edge.

hips and waist shaping
Maintaining patt st, dec 1 st at each side every 6 rows, 4(3, 3, 3) times—57(65, 73, 81) sts rem.
Work even in patt st until piece measures 8(8, 8½, 9) in/20(20, 21.5, 23) cm from CO edge, end after WS row.

back shaping
Maintaining patt st, inc 1 st at each side, every 3 rows, 3 times, and every 4 rows, 1(0, 0, 0) time—65(71, 79, 87) sts.
Work even until piece measures 13½(14, 14½, 15) in/34(35.5, 37, 38) cm from CO edge, end after WS row.

armhole shaping
(RS) BO 6 sts at beg of next 2 rows—56(59, 67, 75) sts.
(RS) Dec 1 st at each end of every other row, 2 times—49 sts.
From here on, work a 2-st garter border (counting the no-longer-necessary selvage st as 1 of the sts at each armhole edge.
Work even in patt st (with border sts) until piece measures 20(20½, 21½, 22½) in/51(52, 54.5, 57) cm, end after a WS row.

neck shaping
(RS) Work 10 sts in patt st (right shoulder), BO 29(35, 43, 51) sts for neck, work 10 sts in patt st (left shoulder).
Leave right shoulder sts on hold.

left shoulder

(WS) Continue with garter st border at armhole edge for remainder of piece. Work 1 row even.

(RS) At neck edge, dec 1, work to end—9 sts rem for shoulder.

Work even as est until piece measures 22½(23, 24, 25) in /57(58, 61, 63.5) cm from CO edge. BO.

right shoulder

With WS facing, join yarn, work as for left shoulder, reversing shaping.

right front

CO 33(35, 39, 43) sts.

Setup Row: Purl.

Row 1: (RS) K2 *K1, yf, sl st purlwise, yb; repeat from * to last two sts, k2.

> **note:** There will be a 2-st garter st border on the nonseam edge of piece (a.k.a. the center front).

Row 2: P to last two sts, k2.

Row 3: K5, *bring yarn to front, sl 1 st, bring yarn to back, k1, repeat from * to last st, k2.

Row 4: P to last two sts, k2.

Repeating these 4 rows makes patt st.

Work even in patt st until piece measures 2½ in/6 cm from edge, end after WS row.

hips and waist shaping

(RS) Maintaining patt st, dec 1 st at seam side (end of RS rows) (i.e., the side without the garter border) every 6 rows, 4(3, 3, 3) times—29(32, 36, 40) sts rem.

Work even in patt st until piece measures 8(8, 8½, 9) in/20(20, 21.5, 23) cm from edge, end after WS row.

CONTINUED

---

shaping with decreases and increases

Different methods produce different directional decreases. This is important anytime you have to do shaping for something like a waist or neckline. To decrease 1 stitch slanting left, you can use a ssk (slip 1 stitch knitwise, slip a second stitch knitwise, knit both together through the back loop). To decrease 1 stitch slanting right, you can k2tog (knit 2 stitches together). That's all there is to it!

bust shaping

Maintaining patt st, inc 1 st at seam side, every 3 rows 3 times and every 4 rows 1(0, 0, 0) time—33(35, 39, 43) sts rem.

Work even until piece measures 13½(14, 14½, 15) in/34(35.5, 37, 38) cm from edge, end after a RS row.

armhole shaping

(WS) Continuing as est., BO 6 sts, work to end.

(RS) Dec 1 st at armhole edge (end of RS rows) every other row 2 times—25(27, 31, 35) sts rem.

From here on, work a 2-st garter border at armhole end.

Work even in patt st (with border sts) until piece measures 15(15½, 16½, 17½) in/38(39.5, 42, 44.5) cm, end after WS row.

neck shaping

(RS): BO 13(15, 19, 23) sts, work to end in patt st—12 sts rem.

(WS) Work 1 row even.

(RS) Dec 1 st at neck edge every other row 2 times—10 sts rem for shoulder.

right shoulder

Maintaining 2 sts in garter st at *both* ends of the row (neck edge and armhole edge), continue in patt st on rem sts until piece measures 22½(23, 24, 25) in/57(58, 61, 63.5) cm from CO edge. BO.

left front

Work as for Right Front, but reverse shaping by working armhole shaping at beg of RS rows and neck shaping at beg of WS rows.

finishing

Block to measurements.

Using mattress stitch, sew up side and shoulder seams.

Weave in ends.

reverse shaping

I know, I know, sometimes reading "reverse shaping" in a pattern can be frustrating. It's so much better when everything's written out for you, right? Well, my fellow lazy daisies, the fact is that as you get into more advanced patterns you'll tend to run into this more often because those patterns probably already have longer instructions than easier patterns. Space is money in the publishing world, so short(er) is often sweet(er). No worries, though. Just take it line by line: If you have to BO at the beginning of a RS row on the first piece, then you'll BO at the beg of the WS row on the next row. If you did a left-slanting decrease on one piece, then likely you'll do a right-slanting decrease on the second one. Catch my drift?

You've totally got this!

optional

- Hand-sew sequin trim around neckline front edge and front opening edges (see photo, page 124).
- Sew on sequin trim strip to mock a pocket (see photo, page 124).
- Sew on a hook and eye if you want to wear the vest closed, or accessorize with a slim belt.

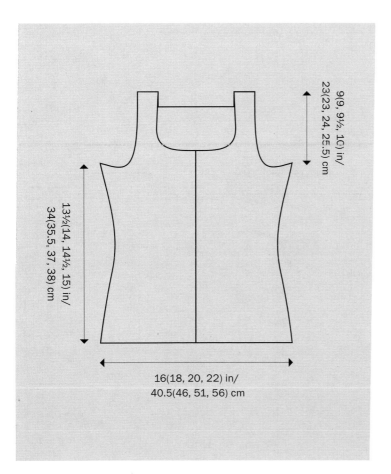

9(9, 9½, 10) in/
23(23, 24, 25.5) cm

13½(14, 14½, 15) in/
34(35.5, 37, 38) cm

16(18, 20, 22) in/
40.5(46, 51, 56) cm

IN THE BAG

BERRY STITCH PURSE

······················

Who needs diamonds? Clearly a good bag is a girl's best friend! This purse is an everyday, vintage-style sack that you begin by working straight and then you switch to rounds. It's quick to knit, using a double strand of yarn, and fun to make because of the no-fuss shaping!

Instructions

note: Hold two strands of yarn together throughout.

base of purse

Using circular needle and with double strand, CO 4 sts.
Row 1: Kf&b, k to last st, kf&b—6 sts.
Row 2: Knit.
Repeat Rows 1 and 2 twice more—10 sts.
Knit every row until piece measures 7 in/18 cm from CO edge.
Row 3: Ssk, k to the last 2 sts, k2tog.
Row 4: Knit.
Rep Rows 3 and 4 twice more—4 sts rem.

body

Using dpns, pick up 50 sts around base. Join—54 sts.

note: You'll now be working in rounds.

Rnds 1–2: Knit.
Rnd 3: Changing to circ, *k1, M1; rep from * around—108 sts.
Rnd 4: Knit.
Rnd 5: *(P1, k1, p1) in the next st, k3tog; rep from * around.
Rnd 6: Purl.
Rnd 7: *K3tog, (p1, k1, p1) in the next st; rep from * around.
Rnd 8: Purl.
Repeat Rnds 5–8 until body measures 9 in/23 cm.
Next Rnd: *K1, k3tog; rep from * around—54 sts rem.

ridge flaps

Find sides and place half the sts on holder—27 sts on needle.
Work in garter st for 3 in/7.5 cm.
BO.
Place sts from holder on needle and work in garter st for 3 in/7.5 cm.
BO.

finishing

Weave in ends.

Optional lining: Place bag onto fabric that's been folded in half. Beginning just under the ridge flaps and adding ½ in/12 mm seam allowance, trace around the bag body and base. Cut fabric out, giving you 2 pieces. With RS together and using ¼ in/6 mm seam allowance (additional allotted allowance is for give), machine-sew or hand-sew the 2 pieces together at sides and bottom.

Fold top edge over so ½ in/12 mm of RS is facing out; press.

Insert lining into bag body. Using sewing needle and thread, hand-tack the folded hem of lining to the body of the bag (the ridge flaps will not be lined).

Attach handle by folding ridge flap over widest point of handle, and then with yarn needle and yarn, whipstitch closed.

Repeat for opposite side.

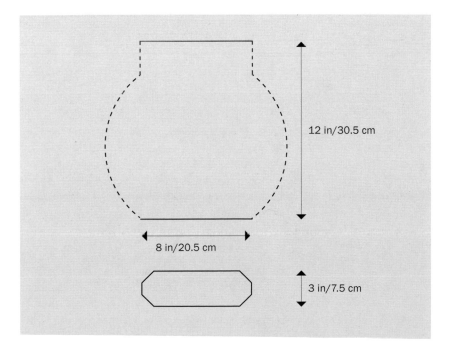

12 in/30.5 cm

8 in/20.5 cm

3 in/7.5 cm

iLACE, uLACE

LACY iPAD SLEEVE

....

I'm one of those knitters who had to ease my way into lace knitting. Sleeves (a.k.a. cozies) are a great way to practice the technique because they offer quick results and display your work cheerfully on the gadget of your choice. This project focuses on knitting lace without a chart, using text only. iLace, uLace, we all knit lace!

SKILLS
Lace Knitting
Single-Crochet Edging
(page 27)

FINISHED MEASUREMENTS
7½ in by 9½ in/
19 cm by 24 cm

YARN
Scraps (approx. 40 yd/36.5 m)
sock-weight yarn

NEEDLES
US 3/2.5 mm needles (or size
needed to obtain gauge)

NOTIONS
Yarn needle
One 1-in/2.5-cm button
Sewing needle
Thread
Size D/3.25 mm crochet hook

GAUGE
22 stitches per 4 in/10 cm
in garter stitch

Instructions

traveling vine stitch pattern
Row 1: (RS) K1, *yo, ktbl, yo, k2tog-tbl, k5; rep from * to last st, k1.
Row 2: P5, *p2tog-tbl, p7; rep from * to last 6 sts, p2tog-tbl, p4.
Row 3: K1, *yo, ktbl, yo, k2, k2tog-tbl, k3; rep from * to last st, k1.
Row 4: P3, *p2tog-tbl, p7; rep from * to last 8 sts, p2tog-tbl, p6.
Row 5: K1, *ktbl, yo, k4, k2tog-tbl, k1, yo; rep from * to last st, k1.
Row 6: P2, *p2tog-tbl, p7; rep from * to end.
Row 7: K6, *k2tog, yo, ktbl, yo, k5; rep from * to last 4 sts, k2tog, yo, ktbl, yo, k1.
Row 8: P4, *p2tog, p7; rep from * to last 7 sts, p2tog, p5.
Row 9: K4, *k2tog, k2, yo, ktbl, yf, k3; rep from * to last 6 sts, k2tog, k2, yo, ktbl, yo, k1.
Row 10: P6, *p2tog, p7; rep from * to last 5 sts, p2tog, p3.
Row 11: K1, *yo, k1, k2tog, k4, yo, ktbl; rep from * to last st, k1.
Row 12: *P7, p2tog; rep from * to last 2 sts, p2.

CO 42 sts.
Rows 1–4: Knit.
Rows 5–172: Work 12 rows in traveling vine stitch pattern, 14 times.
Rows 173–176: Knit.
BO.

finishing

Block to shape.
Single-crochet loosely and evenly along each side of piece to create strong edging for seams.
Weave in ends.
Fold piece in half and seam up sides.

button loop
Using hook and a *double strand* of yarn, join at center of back edge of the piece. Crochet a chain long enough to fit around a button. Sew the end of the chain down to create a loop.
Sew button onto the center of the top edge of the front of piece.

FELT
GOOD

FELTED ZIPPY BAG

....

Sometimes upping the ante on your skills has very little to do with the knitting portion of a project and is all about how you finish it. This Felted Zippy Bag is knit in the round with a simple stockinette stitch and then fancy-fied by machine felting and adding a needle-felted embellishment. When it's over, you'll be a felt master and will be able to say that you Felt Good finishing this bag! This bag is worked in the round, then joined at the lower edge using the 3-needle bind-off method.

Instructions

bag

Beginning at top edge using circ, CO 40 sts. Join, taking care not to twist sts.

Begin St st (knit every round).

Work even until piece measures 15 in/38 cm from CO edge.

BO using 3-needle bind-off method:

Turn piece inside out. Hold circ parallel so half of the bag sts are on one "side" and half on the other. Using the spare needle, BO 2 sts (1 on front needle, 1 on back) at a time by knitting them together; repeat. There'll now be 2 sts on the additional needle; bring the second st over the first to drop it off the needle. Repeat to end.

finishing

Weave in ends.

Turn RS out.

needle felt design

Make a template by photocopying the design on the facing page. With carbon paper and pencil, trace the design onto card stock. Use a craft knife to cut out the design.

Following the Needle Felting directions, needle felt the design onto the bag front, about 1 in/2.5 cm from the top edge.

lining bag

Cut 2 pieces of fabric, each ½ in/12 mm wider and 1¼ in/3 cm longer (higher) than the felted bag.

With RS together and using a ¼-in/6-mm seam allowance, sew sides and bottom.

Fold 1 in/2.5 cm at top edge to WS and press.

Pin zipper to folded top edge of lining.

note: If your zipper's a bit too long, leave the tail end dangling off fabric.

Open the zipper and sew in place, using a zipper foot and a ⅛-in/ 3-mm seam allowance.

With WS facing, insert lining into bag. Tuck excess zipper tail between lining and bag.

Using sewing needle and thread, hand-stitch lining to bag.

Enlarge 200%

felting

Felting isn't an exact science. There's a loose rule of an approximate 30 percent shrinkage rate. However, a few variables can kick that rule to the curb. Different animal fibers felt at different rates, as do similar fibers that are spun differently into yarn. A knitted piece will also shrink more lengthwise than it will widthwise. If you're picky about the actual final size of your FO—that's knit-speak for "finished object"—(like if it needs to fit), then it's imperative that you knit a swatch, measure it, felt it, then measure it again to get an accurate gauge. If you're a knitting wild card—a knitter gone rogue (like myself)— then you'll just blindly take the 30 percent rule as gospel and wing it. I love surprises!

RESOURCES ▶ ▶ ▶ ▶ ▶ ▶ ▶ ▶ ▶ ▶ ▶ ▶ ▶

Yarn Companies

Bernat
Bernat.com

Berroco
Berroco.com

Blue Sky Alpacas
Blueskyalpacas.com

Brooklyn Tweed
Brooklyntweed.net

Knitting Fever (Sublime & Noro)
Knittingfever.com

Lorna's Laces
Lornaslaces.net

Madeline Tosh
Madelinetosh.com

Spud & Chloe
Spudandchloe.com

Knitting Information Sources

Brioche stitch: Briochestitch.com

Clark, Evelyn A. *Knitting Lace Triangles*. Wenatchee, WA: Fiber Trends, 2007.

Howell, Vickie. *Knit Aid: The Learn It, Fix It, Finish It Guide for the Knitter on the Go!* New York: Sterling, 2008.

Knight, Erika, Ed. *Lace & Eyelets: 250 Stitches to Knit*. Loveland, CO: Interweave Press, 2007.

Parry-Jones, Maria. *The Knitting Stitch Bible*. Iola, WI: Krause Publications, 2009.

Vogue Knitting Magazine. *Vogue Knitting Stitchionary*, Vols 1 and 2. New York: Sixth & Spring Books, 2005 and 2006.

INDEX

ACKNOWLEDGMENTS ▶ ▶ ▶ ▶ ▶ ▶ ▶ ▶

First off, I'd like to thank my former editor, Jodi Warshaw, who signed me to do this book, and my current editor Laura Lee Mattingly and assistant Lisa Tauber, who picked up the yarn ball without missing a step! Also, Claire Fletcher, Marie Oishi, Allison Weiner, Steve Kim, and Lorraine Woodcheke from Chronicle Books, and my copy editor Ellen Wheat.

To my friend and photographer Jody Horton and his wonderful staff: Bill Sallans, Kate LeSuer, Eliza Kelly, and Sean Johnson—thanks for hustling in the mud and rain to make this book look purty!

To the former folks at Caron International—Ed Bolen, Jan Kahn, Cari Clement, Frank Jankowski, and the wonderful staff—thank you for being trusting enough to put my face to the Caron name and giving me license to design and run with the yarn line that's used for half of the projects in this book. Another big thanks to Ryan Newell, Mike Feehrer, and Sara Arblaster for seeing the value in the line and bringing it over to the Bernat side of the company. That's what dreams are made of, people!

Thanks to Libby Bailey, Brenda Lewis, Stephanie Mrse, Lolita Whitmore, Renee Barnes and Darlene Dale, the contract knitters whose hours of stitching made the pieces in this book come to life—I couldn't have done it without you! Additionally, I'd like to extend much appreciation to Chris Bahls for his knitting prowess, lace knowledge, and Illustrator wizardry.

On a personal note, a big, mushy thanks to the loves of my life: Dave and Clover Campbell and Tanner and Tristan Howell. Your love, senses of humor, and undying support keep me motivated.

To Mom for being my biggest fan (and most trusted sample knitter) and Debi Campbell for helping with the kids while I finished this book—thankyouthankyouthankyou!

To my besties: Tammy Izbicki and Noelle Corcoran, your sarcasm, loyalty, and love lifts me up where I belong! Wait, what?

The MEOWers, who for the writing of seven books have consistently been there to offer council and show support. I love you all!